CW00666234

HOTWELLS

SPA TO PANTOMIME

Sue Stops

BRISTOL BOOKS

Bristol Books CIC, The Courtyard, Wraxall,
Wraxall Hill, Bristol, BS48 1NA

Hotwells: Spa to Pantomime,
Written and researched by Sue Stops
Edited by Clive Burlton

Published by Bristol Books 2020

ISBN: 9781909446229

Copyright: Sue Stops

Design: Joe Burt

Sue Stops has asserted her right under the Copyright,
Designs and Patents Act of 1988 to be identified as the author of this work.

All rights reserved. This book may not be reproduced or transmitted in any form or in any means without the prior written consent of the publisher, except by a reviewer who wishes to quote brief passages in connection with a review written in a newspaper or magazine or broadcast on television, radio or on the internet.

A CIP record for this book is available from the British Library

Front cover images courtesy of Peter Davey, Hotwells Millennium Exhibition, Liz Marleyne, Symonds Aerial Pictures
and Hotwells Pantomime records. Back cover image courtesy of Peter Davey.

Bristol Books CIC is a not-for-profit Community Interest Company that publishes important and untold stories about lives, communities, places and events that have significance and interest in Bristol and the surrounding area.

CONTENTS

INTRODUCTION

'Hang on 'til we get to Hotwells!' 'Where's Hotwells?' 'It's a bit of Bristol'. This first introduction to Hotwells, came in the 1940s on a car journey from Bridgwater to Coventry to visit grand-parents and later when, as a treat, the family visited Alfred the gorilla and Rosie the elephant at Bristol Zoo. A very convenient public toilet on the main road alongside the harbour (you could park outside) was the answer to a prayer.**

Around 20 years later, as a newly qualified teacher at Bedminster Down School, I moved into a truly grotty flat in Cornwallis Crescent. I got married from there and moved into an even more dilapidated flat in Royal York Crescent rented for £2 4/d a week. After a few years living in the country in the idyllic village of Queen Charlton there was a hankering to return to Clifton and Hotwells where friends seemed to be enjoying an exciting lifestyle. Desire became reality and for 40 years Freeland Place became home.

This book, in three parts, looks at the community of Hotwells and Cliftonwood and how it has learnt to cope with some extraordinary changes. Imagine, in the early 1800s, having to cope with 1,000 men digging the massive pit that would become Cumberland Basin, or the distress of the community in the 1960s when the road system over the basin involved destroying the heart of Hotwells to enable cars to become more important than people.

Part One tells a brief history of Hotwells and Cliftonwood as part of the much wider area of Clifton.

Part Two tells the story of how the community in the late 1970s, restored Hope Chapel as Hope Centre and ran it as a Community Arts Centre for 20 years. As Hope Chapel it had served the local community since the 18th century days of the Spa but in the 1970s faced demolition.

Part Three celebrates the Annual Pantomime which started at Hope Centre and which, as the biggest annual Community event in Hotwells and Cliftonwood, reached its 40th Anniversary in 2020.

This book was almost finished when news arrived that plans are afoot for more changes round the Cumberland Basin. Among the streets knocked down when the 'Flyover' was built, was Western Square. One can only hope that this is the inspiration for the name 'Western Harbour' and the ideas that planners have for Hotwells. Of course, there will be change. It is inevitable as new generations bring new ideas and life to an established area but, hopefully, they will learn from the experiences of older generations and have respect for the rich heritage they have responsibility to care for. Many of the people with memories of the 1960s have died but heaven help anyone who has to go through all that again!

Experiences over more than 300 years, ensure that the lively Community Association together with local 'feisty' people, are ready to cope with whatever life throws at them.

Martin Parr's Millennium community photograph. Twice it poured with rain but this was third time lucky!

Cumberland Basin locks
under construction,
about 1808 (Painting
by G Holmes).

A BRIEF HOTWELLS HISTORY

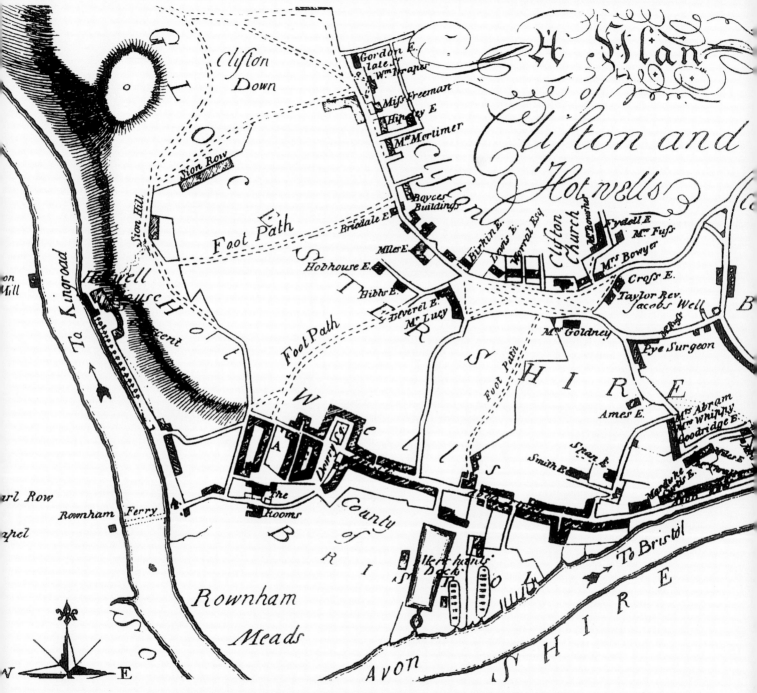

Mr Hill's map of Clifton 1787, showing the growth of Merchants houses in Clifton.

EARLY HOTWELLS

BEFORE YOU START TO READ
Historically the whole area is Clifton. Hotwells was developed first as a Spa during the 18th century but was closely followed by Clifton. Clifton Wood (Cliftonwood from now on) is accessed by just two roads and was developed during the mid-1800s in a wood beneath Goldney. The name 'Hotwells' in this book refers to both Hotwells and Cliftonwood.

The Society of Merchant Venturers knew exactly what they were doing when, towards the end of the 17th century, they bought most of the two manors of Clifton. They became owners of rough farmland near the rolling downs which would eventually become Clifton and the rocky slopes down to the beautiful Gorge and River Avon to what would become Hotwells and Cliftonwood. The Merchants wanted to move well away from their homes and businesses round the harbour in central Bristol where it was dirty, noisy, rough and bawdy, and sought to build 'garden' houses where there was peace and quiet and fresh air. Clifton was just what they were after. They also had their eye on the strange hot spring which bubbled up from the River Avon in the gorge near to where the lower station of Clifton Rocks Railway is today. This had been attracting a growing number of visitors including Queen Catherine of Braganza in 1677, who believed the water could help with their aches and pains. Stories of miraculous cures abounded. The shrewd Merchants saw the area as an investment opportunity and wanted to develop the new area of Hotwells into a fashionable spa like those at Buxton, Cheltenham and Bath.

Building began in Clifton where grand mansions with enviable views appeared at the top of the hill. The Goldneys, the Farrs, the Fishers and other merchants built fine houses some of which are now owned by the University of Bristol and used for student accommodation. They got the gardens they longed for and Thomas Goldney created a masterpiece complete with a grotto which displayed quartz crystals known as Bristol Diamonds. Down the hill, the tidal River Avon, Bristol's disgusting open sewer, flowed through the spectacular gorge. Early pictures show few dwellings along the river, so work began on 'new builds'. The money to fund the work came from land leased or sold to developers, the very land which the Merchants had acquired with profits from trading. Sad to say much of this came from involvement in the lucrative, albeit horrific slave trade which, disgracefully, was not abolished until 1833. Even then the compensation paid for a slave's freedom would be further invested in local businesses.

In 1695 two merchants, Thomas Callowhill and Charles Jones, linen draper and soap boiler respectively, were granted a 90-year lease from the Merchants for the Hot Well but had to provide secure enclosure for the spring, together with a pump room, to ensure the water was not contaminated by the river. Once that happened the Spa's popularity rocketed. Lodgings were urgently needed for the growing number of visitors and a fine Assembly Room was built in 1723. Directories of the time give some idea of what went on as the Spa grew in popularity, but much is left to the imagination. How did they manage without electricity, running water, computers or phones? There was no TripAdviser to guide visitors or Tourist Information Centres. What's more, the whole area had no roads, just rough tracks. So, what was so special

ABOUT THE WELL AND THE WATER

There were several wells in Hotwells, hence the name. The spring of water gushed out at about 60 gallons (273 litres) a minute at around 76 degrees Fahrenheit (24C) from the base of St Vincent's Rock nearly under the Clifton Suspension Bridge. It was revealed at low tide but at high tide, the River Avon's water which came from Bristol's stinking sewers covered and totally contaminated it. The spring water needed to be protected from the river water before the public were allowed near it.

Over the years it was thought to be efficacious when drunk to help ailments described as 'pimply faces' and 'feeble brains' as well as serious, life threatening illnesses such as cancer and tuberculosis, better known as consumption. It could be drunk or used for just about anything and was in great demand. Fifteen glass-houses produced bottles for the water which was transported all over the country. Some went abroad on sailing ships. Many scientists analysed

Matthews's New History of Bristol or Complete Guide and Bristol Directory 1793-1794, tells most of what is known about the Spa days. It is a delight to read but sometimes difficult. Here he describes the gorge and woods. Try saying this quickly! "The ear is delighted with the melodious notes and with the morning or evening fongs of a thoufand feathered fongfters."

the water and the conclusion appears to be that it was satisfactory spa water but contained nothing magical to explain the claimed cures. However, the doctors concluded that if a person thought it was doing him/her some good, then that was all one can ask.

The spring no longer exists because the rocks were blown up in the late 1800s to enable ships the size of the SS Great Britain to navigate the river more easily. Sadly, Bristol lost its famous spa water.

The late Fred Wedlock – local folk singer, broadcaster and entertainer – saved the last known bottle from the General Draper pub on Hotwell Road before it was demolished.

about the well water?

Architects, William and Thomas Paty, designed many of the terraces to ensure an economical use of land with good profits for the builders. Externally the houses in a particular terrace would appear similar whilst internally almost all were built to the same 'five floor design'. The basement was where the work was done. The ground floor, first and second floors were to let as a whole or as rooms. Servants lived in the attics. Dowry Square and Chapel Row (1721) were among the early lodging houses while Albemarle Row and Dowry Parade appeared in 1763

when the Spa was at its liveliest.

However, despite all the talented architects, builders and craftsmen, nobody, absolutely nobody, appears to have taken on board the basic need for a reliable water supply and efficient disposal of waste. The river Avon stank, and the people stank. Perhaps it was all so awful, nobody noticed!

Records fail to show exactly how many visitors came between April and September each year but there were hundreds, some of whom were day-trippers from Bath. They appear to fit into three groups. There was the 'perfectly fit' group, there to have a good time. These were well-off socialites with good connections who might be described as 'posh'. The 'off colour' group were hoping something in the water would lead to recovery while the 'desperately sick' were ready to try anything and were prepared to stay for as long as necessary. This makes for a strange mix of clients at the Spa. One thing is certain. They all 'took the waters'. For the fit it was the fashionable thing to do and, fortified by a visit to the pump room, the well-heeled, be-wigged society people joined in activities such as dancing, painting in Leigh Woods and going to concerts. Some visited Mr. Hippesley's Theatre at Jacob's Wells, Mr. Goldney's Grotto or the short-lived Vauxhall Gardens. There was flirting, playing cards, boating on the river, gossiping, dressing up, trying on wigs, making up and sticking on beauty spots. A visit to 'Dr Downs' to ride horses (sometimes two on a horse) provided exercise and public breakfasts were greatly enjoyed. Life was a ball! Those feeling 'off colour' were ready to try anything that might help their symptoms but were not too ill to join in the fun. For the very sick it was more serious and doctors, quacks, and apothecaries devised regimes for taking the water which might, or might not, do them any good at all. Part of the cure was believing that it might help. These very varying needs meant that some lodging houses were care homes with landladies who knew little more about caring for the sick than the quack doctors. Undertakers made fortunes and a Stranger's Burial Ground catered for visitors who died away from home. The sheer logistics of ensuring everyone was cared for and had a good time is astonishing.

Local people kept the Spa going. Almost without exception landladies ran the lodging houses but, of course, there were coachmen and ostlers, doctors and apothecaries, builders, bakers and candle makers (not forgetting the odd stick maker!). Washer women were always busy. Grocers visited regular markets for cheese,

Life at the Spa from Emma Marshall's book, Bristol Diamonds or the Hot Wells of the year 1773.

eggs and fish while butchers often had a slaughterhouse round the back. The milkmen unknowingly sold untreated milk – the very cause of the consumption (TB) that so many people were suffering from. The worst job of all, was that of the night-soil men – the horrors of their job are indescribable! There were perukiers, dressmakers, musicians and boatmen. Visitors could read five weekly

DODSHON FOSTER AT ROCK HOUSE

An Account of a Journey to Bristol in the Year 1766, by Dodshon Foster. The diary is in Lancaster Maritime Museum. Below is the entry for the seventh day of his trip on June 7, 1766:

7th day 7th. At Dr Riggs Lodgings before breakfast, he went with me to look at other lodgings, we fixed on 2 rooms at the Rock house a bed in the parlour 15s a lodging room 10s & a Servants room 5s per week—Uncle & Aunt came down with us to the Hot wells about noon, my dear drank 2 glasses of water: in the afternoon I went with Uncle & Aunt to purchase Crockery ware, Groceries, Chocolate Sago &c. which we should want at our lodgings—a Chocolate pot & grater.

newspapers, published on different days. All these independent traders knew that if there was no work, there was no money. One wonders how they managed out of season when only the sick remained.

Food in the eighteenth century was locally sourced, organic, seasonal and sustainable. Clothing was made of cotton, wool, leather, or silk – not a man-made fibre to be seen! Power came from the sun, water, wind, horses and man. The wheel has turned.

TWO SPECIAL PLACES

It is important to remember that the Spa WAS Hotwells. For more than 100 years the area slowly developed into the Hotwells of today. For much of the time it was a building site as one well-designed terrace after another appeared, the very ones that still exist today. Smaller buildings, shops, businesses and cottages filled in the spaces left, adding to the ultimate charm of the whole area. Buildings outlast many generations and all have a different story to tell. Two buildings have seen all the changes, for good or bad that have happened and survive today.

ROCK HOUSE

Rock House, on the Hotwell Road, was built in the late 17th century and was probably the first lodging house to be built. Popular because it was just a stone's throw across the Piazza, to the Hotwell House which was central to all that went on. The Piazza was a meeting place and a parking area for carriages and horses (a problem even then!). Eventually, the Colonnade was built in 1786 providing shops and a covered way from Rock House to the Pump Room. 'The Diary of Dodshon Foster' was recently published by Lancaster Maritime Museum. Foster, a merchant who owned ships engaged in the slave trade, describes the trials and tribulations of getting from Lancaster to Hotwells with his sick wife. His account includes descriptions of coaching inns where they stayed, how long each part of the journey took and what it cost.

Hotwell House c1696 would have been where the disused bottom station of Clifton Rocks Railway c1893 is shown on the left. The Colonnade c1786 was a shopping arcade with lodgings above which linked Hotwell House to Rock House, the first of the lodging houses and the most important. In front of them, over the Hotwell Road lie the disused and rotting landing stages from the days of the P & A Campbell paddle steamers.

He talks about the relief of hiring accommodation at Rock House, of finding a maid and obtaining food. His immense concern for his sick wife is evident as he constantly mentions her production of stools! Rock House still stands proudly beside the Hotwell Road today and is probably the most important building remaining from the glory days of the Spa.

HOPE CHAPEL

The other building, Hope Chapel, is central to this story, and was built towards the end of the popularity of the Spa.

In 1772 Willielma Campbell, Viscountess Glenorchy (1741-1784) met Lady Henrietta Hope (1750-1786) of Hopetoun, a huge mansion near Edinburgh. The ladies, both evangelical Christians, became friends but were probably suffering from symptoms of consumption when they visited Hotwells to take the water. While there they

decided to build a chapel and Lady Hope gave £2,500 towards the cost. There are two reasons suggested as to why they felt moved to do this. First of all it was a long slog up uphill to St. Andrew's Church in Clifton for two frail ladies although a Chapel had been built in Dowry Square. Another suggestion was that they were extremely shocked by the goings-on at the Spa and wanted to redress the balance. Lady Hope died in January 1786 and her friend who named the chapel after her, died later the same year. An executor saw the job finished. The name 'Hope' crops up several times round Hotwells; there's Hope Chapel on Hope Chapel Hill, next to Hope Square. There was even a Hope School Room.

The Chapel belongs to the Congregational Federation and has been in continuous use since 1786. However, in the 1990s the congregation became too small and they were forced to disband but the chapel was not deconsecrated. There have been many changes in Hotwells but Hope Chapel has survived them all probably because of its unique position on Hope Chapel Hill. The biggest change came in the 1970s when it was scheduled for demolition, along with Hope Square and Freeland

Hope Chapel with graves in front of the building.

Place, to make way for flats, but you will have to wait until later in this story to see what happened.

THE SPA DAYS COME TO AN END

The Spa lasted from the late 17th century to the close of the 18th century. The end came quickly when the lease ran out, and the Society of Merchant Venturers was forced to spend its own money to bring things up to scratch. In 1790 Samuel Powell took on the tenancy of the Spa and improved things, but charges were increased so much that it priced itself out of business. Times were changing anyway and William Pennington who had become the Beau Nash of Hotwells, complete with gold medal, did his best to liven things up but it had had its day. The situation abroad was fraught, and anyway, the King had decided that the seaside was infinitely more desirable than a Spa. Within a short time, everything changed, the Socialites left and only the suffering sick people remained. Oh – and all the beautiful terraces and houses that still make Hotwells such a great place to live.

However, it was not quite the end. The Hotwell House was demolished in 1822 but in 1850 a Mr Bolton, entrepreneur, took a chance and built a new Hotwell House complete with baths and a shop selling intriguing souvenirs Sadly, the venture never took off and that building was demolished in 1867 when the Port and Pier Railway was established between Avonmouth and Bristol docks.

For those still wanting to take the water a special pump was installed in a grotto near the lower station of Clifton Rocks Railway. This was discontinued for health and safety reasons.

THE SCIENTISTS LAUGHING GAS AND FOSSILS

When the Socialites stopped coming to the Spa the place lost its appeal. Many consumptives were among the sick who were left behind and it became the saddest and most depressing place. Confidence in the Spa water waned and in 1793, Dr Beddoes decided that perhaps the cure for consumption might be in the air, not water. He began experimenting with gases in some peculiarly odd ways. By 1799 he had set up the Pneumatic Institute at 11 Dowry Square and was working with patients using Nitrous Oxide, better known as laughing gas. His assistants were the brilliant Humphry Davy and Peter (Thesaurus) Roget. Beddoes was also a poet and interested in literature and their group of friends included poets Coleridge and Southey who greatly enjoyed sampling the nitrous oxide. Who said that life was dull in Hotwells?

As well as being scientists and poets they collected fossils, many from Dundry. The Age of Enlightenment was a time when people began to question how, for example, fossils, fitted into the Biblical story of the Creation. People began to question their beliefs.

Dowry Parade was home to James Johnson, a tinman with a considerable fortune which he spent acquiring a vast collection of fossils. His house was jam-packed full of them. At the sale following his death in 1844, ichthyosaur fossils sold for large sums and went to the great museums such as the Natural History Museum in London. Many went to the Bristol Institution, later the Bristol City Museum where the collection was destroyed by enemy bombing during World War Two. One huge fossil, part of an ichthyosaur, which had been discovered at Lyme Regis by Mary Anning, survived. It is in the collection and sometimes displayed. James Johnson left a large fortune. He also wrote a book as he was Guardian of the Poor.

A MASSIVE DIGGING PROJECT!

After the Spa building boom, it would be reasonable to expect a break in activity. Not so! Bristol, an inland port on a tidal river, was losing trade to the port of Liverpool which had expanded rapidly and was winning business from the City. What did the City need to do? There is a saying that nothing gets done in Bristol but on this occasion it was, if rather too late. William Jessop put forward plans in 1802 to create a 'floating harbour' (1803-09) by diverting the

'Rownham Ferry' by Rolinda Sharples 1822. The whereabouts of this painting is unknown. The people depicted are all her friends crossing on the ferry to enjoy tea at Long Ashton. Samuel Plimsoll would have had 40 fits!

River Avon round the existing harbour along the 'Cut' which conveniently forms the parish boundary between Hotwells and Southville. Cumberland Basin, hewn out of Rownham Mead, was built to hold a number of big ships. Houses in the Sandford and Oldfield Road area, often known as the 'Island' were built on the spoil. Entrance Lock and Junction Lock (1809) are still in everyday use and water levels are controlled at Underfall Yard. All this was necessary to combat the ceaseless rise and fall of the tide in the docks which made loading and unloading ships problematic. It was incredibly hard work using mostly manpower although gunpowder was used to shift some of the rocks. Around 1,000 navvies were the diggers – no JCBs then! In 1809 the river was successfully diverted and to celebrate, the 1,000 workers who had made Hotwells their home and brought business to the increasing number of traders on Hotwell Road were treated to a huge party. Food and a gallon of beer for every man plus a riot gave all concerned a great night out.

By this time although the first of the Spa lodging houses were already needing attention other terraces such as Clifton Vale, Camden Terrace, the Polygon, and Cornwallis Crescent were completed and infilling with smaller buildings was happening rapidly. Business and trades people were establishing themselves on the Hotwell Road.

Things were on the up.

An aerial view of the Georgian and Victorian Terraces. Most have five storeys. Hope Chapel just appears next to the Polygon (bottom left).

FROM VICTORIAN TIMES TO THE 1950S

Queen Victoria, born in 1819, reigned from **1837 to 1901.** During this time the population of Hotwells increased rapidly as the effects of both the Agrarian and the Industrial revolutions kicked in. The demand for housing, food and clothing was huge but most of all people wanted jobs. Distraught families arrived from the country where they had been forced to leave a tied cottage as machinery took over the farming jobs previously done by horses and men. There was work for some in the shipyards and supporting industries such as sail and rope making but the large number of workers looking for a limited number of jobs did not add up and many families faced a life of poverty. Women found work in service for better off people. The poorest lived in fear of the workhouse. All available apartments and rooms were let with large families sharing just one, maybe two, rooms. The courts behind the shops on the Hotwell Road were dire and the lack of a proper water supply and sewage disposal arrangements, together with a poor diet, led to an outbreak of cholera in 1832. Air pollution caused by fires fuelled with coal, some from the Bedminster collieries was responsible for many respiratory illnesses.

Cliftonwood was the fastest growing community in the area during the mid -1800s. Victorian family-sized, terraced houses, such as those in Ambra Vale, Southernhay and Cliftonwood Crescent were built on the hillside below Goldney. Their proximity to the harbour and new workplaces in the City Centre made them attractive buys. Many were rented out. This compact community, squashed between Clifton and Hotwells and accessed by just two roads, became well established. The colourfully painted houses were originally rather dull and it was only recently when paint manufacturers used modern technology to produce brightly coloured paints that they took on a new personality. Sadly, there is no other historical reason for this to have happened.

In 1860, Susannah Winkworth, a philanthropist

Hope Chapel School Room next door to Hope Chapel was demolished without warning. It could have become a useful meeting room for the community.

concerned about the appalling living conditions in Hotwells, had two houses in Dowry Square repaired, to be let to 'poor but decent' people who could pay regular rent. To show her commitment to those in need she later commissioned a block of flats at Jacob's Wells which had gas and running water. These paved the way for modern Council Flats built in the 1950s. Susannah set a great example as did Hannah Moore who campaigned ceaselessly for the Abolition of Slavery. In later life Hannah moved to Windsor Terrace where she died in 1833. Sarah Haberfield 1798-1874 enabled almshouses for older people to be built on Joy Hill. Haberfield House now overlooks the 'Flyover' and replaced the Gloucester Hotel, well known in the days of the Spa for its turtle soup.

Churches and Chapels were very busy in the 19th century providing a religious, social and caring centre for families although it was mostly the women and children who took advantage of this. The men preferred the camaraderie of the pubs – of which there were many. Services at Hope Chapel were packed and in 1851 congregations of between 600 to 800 people were commonplace. High spots of the year were the Christian festivals and anniversaries but children particularly enjoyed the annual Sunday School Outings to Leigh Woods or the Downs. It would be some years before trains or charabancs took them to Weston-super-Mare. The large school room next to Hope Chapel operated as Clifton Congregational School with 300 children on the roll being taught the '3 Rs' but after 1870, when education became compulsory for children aged five to 13, more emphasis was put on the religious side of things. Trinity Church also provided a school for infants. When not at school children lived a feral life round the docks and the gorge, both very dangerous places. They became streetwise and opportunist very quickly. Boys with behavioural problems at a risk of getting into trouble attended the Industrial School, opened on the Hotwell Road in 1859.

Victorian engineering and innovation arrived with the brilliant Isambard Kingdom Brunel who had been working on

REV FREDERICK BROWN

Born in Kent and a scholar of the Bristol Theological Institute, Rev Frederick W Brown became pastor at Hope Chapel in 1882 after spells preaching in Oldland Common and at Kingsland Chapel, St Phillips. He was well-liked and the Bristol Magpie described him thus in an article in 1884:

As a preacher he is always fresh and forceful; extemporaneous in delivery, every sermon gives due sign of fitting preparation. He is a master of alliteration, and with a copious vocabulary is vigorous and fluent. Evangelical in doctrine, and fervent in spirt, he has always been welcome in the many anniversary services of the neighbourhood, as well as esteemed and useful in his own pulpit. Our earnest hope is that he is yet far from what he himself calls a 'saintly sunset.'

What a nice chap he sounded. Rev Brown married Redland's Sophia Martin in January 1896 and the sun did finally set on his ministerial work when he left Hope Chapel in 1899 after 17 years in the pulpit. The local community rallied around and presented him with £100 to bid him farewell. A tidy sum in 1899 and worth around £12,000 in today's money.

the Great Western Railway. In 1837 the SS Great Western was launched to be followed in 1843 by the screw propelled SS Great Britain. Crowds turned out for the launching and it is said that a shower of rain caused hundreds of umbrellas to be opened over spectators on Brandon Hill causing it to look as if the hill itself was sheltering. Clifton Suspension Bridge opened on December 8, 1864 to great rejoicing but without doubt, the most important thing Brunel achieved for Hotwells was his idea for getting rid of the GREAT STINK that arrived with construction of the Float. He probably couldn't stand it either!

By the mid-19th century most of the big terraces were complete including Cornwallis Crescent, the Polygon, Clifton Vale and Freeland Place. Victoria Terrace bears the Queen's name and Prince Albert is commemorated with the Albert Hall in Green Street. Stabling was still needed for horses some of which pulled trams at the turn of the century, but it was the sight of cars on new roads that started dreams of the freedom that ownership of one could bring. Trade on the Hotwells Road was very busy and it was said that anything and everything needed from birth until the undertaker took over, could be bought there.

The harbour was busy with big ships arriving and leaving on every tide. Among the imports were wine, cattle and tobacco. By the end of the century smoking had increased so much that the three Bonded Warehouses (1905, 1908 and 1919) were built where the huge imports of tobacco were stored before being sent to W.D. & H.O Wills tobacco factories in East Street Bedminster or Raleigh Road in Southville - once the tax had been paid.

At the turn of the 19th century life was better for many and to everyone's delight in around 1893, P & A Campbell Limited arrived from Scotland with paddle steamers which brought fun and pleasure to thousands of people on day trips up and down the Bristol Channel. What is more, in 1893 Clifton Rocks Railway opened and carried people up to Clifton and back down again.

The Girls Sewing Class from Mr Hardy's photograph album.

The Mothers at Tyntesfield, including Mrs G A Gibbs and Rev E Walters, from Mr Hardy's photograph album.

CRUISING INTO THE 20TH CENTURY 1900 – 1918

It was all go in Hotwells in the early 20th century. Baltic Wharf was particularly busy as cargoes of wood arrived regularly from the Baltics and was stored in sheds at the timber yards on Cumberland Road. Local people were never fazed to hear foreign languages spoken in the local shops when crew members from foreign ships went shopping. Ships were still being built and Stotherts had a large boiler making business at Poole's Wharf.

A scene from around 1910, showing the Cliftonwood slopes in the background; three Campbell's paddle steamers; the Royal Navy Reserve ship *Daedalus* and passengers on the Mardyke Ferry.

In 1911 a Working Men's Hostel and Coffee Tavern was built from Number 20 – 24 on the Hotwell Road with beds for 150. The war may well have put paid to this because by 1919 it had become part of Hall and Fitzgerald, a busy factory supplying pipes and accessories for the smoking trade. Mardyke and Gas Ferries took workers across the river to the Wills factories in Bedminster.

Mr Hardy, Church warden of St. Peters at Jacob's Wells was a keen photographer and documented Church events such as the women's visit to Tyntesfield to take tea with Mrs Gibbs. Women's fashion still required long dresses with very big, flowery hats on special occasions, but few had much money to spare. Times were still hard.

At Hope Chapel a Company of the Boy's Brigade was formed. No one dared to complain about the noise when the band practised in the School Room, as their leader lived next door at 1 The Polygon. Churches had football teams and a good footballer might play for several teams, some in the Downs League. Cycling was very popular and groups, usually of men, formed friendly clubs and went off exploring the countryside (and the pubs) at weekends. Three schools served the area, one in the fine Assembly Room left over from Spa days.

WORLD WAR 1, 1914 – 1918

War was looming and broke out in 1914. 'Your Country Needs You' shouted Lord Haig from the hoardings. Thousands of young men joined up not knowing at all what they would experience before it ended in 1918. At the end of May 1914, the Bristol International Exhibition opened on land across the river from Hotwells between Clanage Road and what is now Brunel Way. It was known as White City because of the white plasterboard panels used in constructing the buildings, but only a replica of Bristol Castle had been painted. A cross between a trade and industry fair and a theme park, it should have been a winner, but it was doomed to fail not only because of the political situation. With the onset of war in August 1914 the event was in the throes of being wound up having made a considerable loss. The Colston Hall became one of the local wartime recruitment centres and, believe it or not, the temporary timber buildings at the Exhibition site became a barracks with some recruits boasting that they were living in Bristol Castle.

Hotwells Road, Bristol.

A tram passes the shops demolished when Hillsborough Flats were built in the 1930s The Bear pub was a Coaching Inn.

With the men away, women did the men's work with skill, commitment and humour feeling that they were doing something useful. They enjoyed the busy fun of the workplace and it came as a shock when the men returned home and their jobs were handed back to them.

It was a horrendous time for all those who served in the armed forces and their families and on behalf of the community, on Remembrance Sunday, a wreath is laid on the cross in St Andrew's Churchyard in Clifton.

BETWEEN THE WARS, 1918 – 1939

The Great Depression spread from America and reached Great Britain. Great crowds turned out at Hope Chapel in March 1925 to hear Catherine Booth-Clibborn, known as the Marechale. An evangelical Christian, like Lady Hope, she was the eldest daughter of William Booth, founder of the Salvation Army.

But... it was the 1920s and skirts were shorter! Smoking was all the rage although it was a time when people took 'keep fit' very seriously. There was tennis on the courts along the Portway, and swimming at Jacob's Wells baths. Groups went rambling and cycling was the in thing. Congregations from the churches and chapels

enjoyed charabanc outings to celebrate the choir or the Mothers' Union. The Methodists opened Guest Houses for holidays. It was a time of 'Carry on Camping' and Hotwells Boys Club did just that. This great club – think older teenagers – met at Trinity Church, then moved to the Albert Hall behind the Church Army premises in Dowry Square. They enjoyed social evenings, performed plays, enjoyed snooker and cards, went camping and there was a football team. Girls often joined in, couples fell in love and some got married. It was very successful. Many members joined the forces and were welcomed back when on leave. Good times continued after the war and such was its success that the club bought Grenville Methodist Church School Room (now Bristol Bridge Club)

The back of Ellenborough Buildings in the 1930s with a children's race about to start.

as its HQ. Sadly the club folded in the 1960s and the proceeds from the sale of its premises were donated to Bedminster Down Boys Club.

Campbell's Steamers were seasonal employers with jobs on offer. One involved creating a line round each steamer with real gold leaf, kept for safety under the decorator's bed! The Hotwells pubs including the General Draper were especially busy on Sundays when pubs in Wales were closed. Steamers would bring groups from Cardiff or Barry who would disembark, head straight for the nearest pub and stay there until the steamer was

Men's Cycling Club from Holy Trinity 1930s. Photo from the late Valerie Maggs.

Hotwells Boys Club 1939 outside the Albert Hall. Photo from the late Maurice Mitchell.

ready to take them home.

Buildings were demolished on the intriguingly named Love Street in order to build Hillsborough flats, opened in 1935 by no less than the Prince of Wales. Some slum clearance, long overdue, saw the end to the hovels on Hotwell Road and derelict cottages on Granby Hill.

WORLD WAR 2, 1939 – 1945

World War 2 broke out in 1939 but this time it was nearer home. Once again, men and women joined up to fight for their country but were always worried about the safety of their families back home. Ration books, were issued and people queued for food. There was blackout, no street-lights, shelters, and sirens and all-clears became part of everyday life. Any spare land was used for growing food and locals 'Dug for Victory' on Cabbage Patch Allotments near the bonded warehouses.

Hotwells was vulnerable and on January 3, 1941, Clifton National School, The Cinema, Axten's Department Store, and most heart-breaking of all, Holy Trinity Church were destroyed. In the Good Friday raid a few months later,

CERTIFICATE OF APPRECIATION

Presented to the people of the Hotwells in appreciation of your many acts of kindness to me when I was in Bristol in 1944-1945

James T "Jimmy" Barr

Heber Denty's wood yards were also destroyed. Like many communities in Bristol local people were devastated but again, pulled together. St. Andrew's Church had been closed but was re-opened as a replacement for Holy Trinity, pending the latter's reconstruction. The council provided basic air-raid shelters, but many sought safety in the Portway Tunnel which had no facilities. It was damp, dark and unhealthy, yet people preferred to be there 'because they felt safer under rock'. Those sheltering never forgot the experience but were jealous of the lucky ones who enjoyed slightly more comfort in Clifton Rocks Railway where the BBC had emergency studios and transmitters. Children carried gas masks which they were scared to put on and some were evacuated. The stress felt by the teachers who were themselves scared and worried about their own families was exceptional. Even after raids the schools opened for those left behind. Local resident Marion Roach told stories of how she and her friends had the most wonderful time playing in the dangerous

Received by the Roach family from James Barr, a GI stationed at White City 1944-45.

Coronation celebrations June 2, 1953. Brunswick Place and Caroline Place on either side of the party-goers were demolished when the Flyover was built in the mid-1960s. The Rose of Denmark public house seen in the background, escaped.

ruins and never got told off. Hope Chapel survived and supported the community throughout the war as did other places of worship. The people who experienced the horrors of World War 2 say they will never forget it but recognised that such dreadful events had brought out the best in community spirit.

The war in Europe ended in May 1945 and you could be forgiven for thinking that that would be the end of troubles for Hotwells. The country was bankrupt and there was no money left to spend on improving life for everyone. Spirits were lifted on November 20, 1947 when the Royal Wedding of Elizabeth and Philip Mountbatten took place at Westminster Abbey and Hotwells celebrated with street parties somewhat restricted by on-going food rationing.

As well as war damage, downright neglect was responsible for a lot of dereliction and the old story of absentee landlords not caring for their property rang true. Everywhere in Bristol, from Clifton to Bedminster, from Fishponds to Redland, the streets and houses were run-down, dreary and dismal. Hotwells looked unloved. There had been a hint of things to come but...

CHANGE WAS IN THE AIR!

Flags were flying and street parties lifted spirits. The Coronation of Queen Elizabeth ll took place at Westminster Abbey on June 2, 1953. Black and white pictures spoilt by interference were watched by millions on extremely small TV sets. It was mind-blowing for many. The community began to experience misplaced optimism.

However, fewer ships were using the harbour and local workers were badly affected as new docks at Avonmouth started taking trade, and jobs, from Bristol. The knock-on effect hurt the shopkeepers and traders on Hotwell Road and some closed. The Churches and Chapels were all experiencing falling congregations and, as people no longer saw them as the centre of their social life, some were sold or redeveloped. School rooms were also sold for redevelopment and community resources were lost. People were changing. Why? One reason is that they were better informed. Everyone had a radio and TV ownership was on the horizon. The longed-for car became more affordable and offered a new sense of freedom. People no longer felt tied to the local community and found interests elsewhere. Eventually only Hope Chapel and Holy Trinity survived as places of worship and even they had falling congregations.

Clifton National School was not rebuilt and children were transferred to Hotwells Primary School which also took the young children from Dowry School; they had been using the fine Georgian Assembly Room left from the days of the Spa. In the mid-1950s Ashton Park school at Bower Ashton opened as a bilateral, soon to become a comprehensive school. Because of the 'bulge' (children born after the war) an annex was opened in Beauley Road in Southville. Brown's Café, near the Nova Scotia was a calling point for children walking to school who were given scraps of food which they fed to the timber yard cats on the way. Brown's Café and bakery served local people, transport workers, employees from Underfall and the timber yards, as well as the bonded warehouses. On Good Friday queues stretched right along Merchants Road waiting for Hot Cross Buns.

Life in Hotwells was going on as normal and everything seemed to be recovering after the war but nothing prepared the community for the bombshell about to land...

Wedding of Mr and Mrs Stacey outside Hope Chapel in the 1950s.

An anniversary picture outside Hope Chapel in the 1950s.

Hotwells Boys Club at camp in the 1950s. Photo from the late Maurice Mitchell.

HOTWELLS BEFORE THE WRECKING BALL

Many of the buildings in this photo were demolished when the Flyover was built.

1. **Rownham Inn**
2. **The Brethren Chapel**
3. **Sopey Park**
4. **Anderson's workshop**
5. **Public lavatories**
6. **Territt Memorial Hall**
7. **Spa Assembly Rooms**
8. **Brunel's Swivel Bridge** (survived)

REGENERATION: THE NIGHTMARE OF CUMBERLAND BASIN, 1963-1965

During the 1950s and 1960s regeneration after the war was in full swing. Countrywide, planners had grandiose ideas for developments mainly designed to cope with the expected increase in the number of cars on the road. Bristol was no exception and many listed buildings were pulled down in readiness for planned road works. Local people were horrified to discover what was in store for Hotwells and Cliftonwood which involved the construction of 'The Plimsoll Swing Bridge and road system at Cumberland Basin 1963-65.' Hotwells called it 'the 'Flyover' so that is what it will be referred to here. Someone remarked 'they poor devils dug it all out in the eighteen 'undreds and now they wants to fly over it'. The building work resulted in total chaos for several years before it opened in 1965 having destroyed the disappointed close-knit community.

TOP ROW: February 4, 1963 and the visit of Ernest Marples, Minister of Transport, for the inauguration of the Cumberland Basin Bridges Scheme. Marples is joined the Lord Mayor, Leonard Stevenson and far right Gervais Walker and many dignitaries at a very wintry Hotwells. Marples triggers the start of the demolition work and a bulldozer does the rest.

MIDDLE ROW: Wrecking balls and explosives were also used to bring the buildings down. Lorries removed the rubble.

BOTTOM ROW: The flyover taking shape with huge pillars and massive bridge sections being manoeuvred into place. Far right and on April 14, 1965 with the flyover now constructed, new Transport Minister, Tom Fraser is in the first car to cross the bridge and formally open the Cumberland Basin Bridges Scheme.

Why was it necessary and what was involved? The ever increasing flow of traffic into the city was just too great for the infrastructure of roads and bridges. The Portway (1926) brought traffic from the North, through the stunning gorge into the city. This necessitated removal of the Port and Pier Railway which had linked the Port of Avonmouth with the Port of Bristol. Unfortunately this passed Point House, home of George George of the Gorge. As one of the demolition squad the poor fellow had to demolish his own home! More destruction took place later when the road was widened in 1965 to ease access to the Flyover. The popular General Draper pub was sacrificed along with a number of shops, houses and a chapel.

Meanwhile traffic from the South was increasing rapidly. To get to the city via the Hotwell Road, it crossed the New Cut over the Ashton Swing Bridge which was opened by Lady Smythe in 1906. This ingenious double decker bridge carried trains on the lower level and cars on the upper one. Traffic then crossed the Cumberland Basin at Junction Lock near Dock Cottages. If Junction Lock Bridge was swung Brunel's Swivel Bridge took traffic across the Basin to the road between Brunswick and Caroline Place. The new plans showed that the Flyover would be built near to the Entrance Locks and in order to facilitate this, Caroline, Brunswick and Grenville streets would be totally demolished. Houses, businesses and pubs would go as well as a harbourside walk. Dumbleton's Garage and Anderson's workshop where

Demolition work c1963. This was the site of the Georgian Assembly Room which had served as Dowry School for many years.

wonderful sets of animals were carved for carousels were also doomed. Even the Territt Memorial Hall and public lavatories had to go. It took around five years to complete the transformation and what had been the 'heart and soul' of Hotwells, disappeared for ever. The community remains divided by the Hotwell Road and controlled by the car. Quite disgracefully the Georgian Assembly Room built for visitors to the Spa and used as a primary school, was knocked down. Would this have happened in Bath?

Dame Sylvia Crowe, the renowned landscape architect designed attractive spaces with trees, viewing points and a Piazza which was given to the people of Hotwells in return for their patience during the construction work. In particular she enhanced the stunning view of the slopes and Clifton Suspension Bridge that greet travellers as they approach the Flyover from Ashton. Sadly, there had been little or no consultation about the Piazza or about the rest of the scheme for that matter. The pond with the fountain and the climbing frame had to be dismantled as they were considered dangerous. The café was unsustainable and because the site was not overlooked it became vandalised. It was a great disappointment to local people.

The community wasn't in celebratory mood when the Flyover was opened by the Transport Minister in 1965. One nameless local lady let rip and said what a lot of people were thinking. Everyone had had just about enough. The event was commemorated with a plaque on a large edifice now sited on the cycle path. The cost of £2,500,000 was peanuts in today's money. Was it worth it? The fact is the existing system does work except in rush hours or when somebody has an accident. There are always hold ups when the bridge gets swung for

Shipping in Cumberland Basin during building work on the Flyover c1963/1964.

boats to arrive or depart although the number of ships entering Cumberland Basin has dropped dramatically. The river is rarely dredged and the build-up of mud will inevitably cause flooding. Sadly, the historic grid-iron has completely disappeared under the mud.

Until there is joined-up thinking across the whole region both outside and in Bristol about the huge rise in new housing development and the inevitable increase in the number of cars the problems will increase.

CLIFTON AND HOTWELLS IMPROVEMENT SOCIETY (CHIS), 1964

In 1964 Clifton and Hotwells Improvement Society was formed and began to challenge the City Council about applications which appeared to support inappropriate changes to buildings. This very active group, financed by its membership subscriptions, were involved in one memorable 'clash' when the appalling scheme to build a horrendous eyesore in the Gorge, was rejected. Success built confidence in other local groups to challenge potentially disastrous decisions. They rightly believed that restoration rather than demolition of buildings should be the priority. A group of local people from Hotwells noted that there were plans to demolish Freeland Place, Hope Square and Hope Chapel to be replaced by blocks of flats. The Ottys the Marleynes and others formed a group which protested about the proposed demolition of Hope Square. Eventually there was agreement with the Council that a group of people each willing to buy a house for £2,000 could do so but only if the building had been approved to be wind and water tight first. Just look at Hope Square today!

THE LOCAL COMMUNITY AFTER THE FLYOVER, 1965

Local people, born, raised and married in Hotwells and Cliftonwood, were shocked to discover what life was like in a community divided by a major road. Friends relocated to the new council housing estates in Knowle West, Shirehampton, or Lawrence Weston liked their new homes and gardens but missed their friends and the neighbourliness of Hotwells despite the fact it still looked so run down and unloved after the war. It was fine to have the 'Flyover' looking smart and new; but it was depressing to live in a road where some houses were in serious need of attention. The big terraced houses had fared worst as landlords had neglected them and wanted to get rid of them. Parking problems on Hotwell Road hit traders hard and some decided to call it a day. Even Campbell's Steamers could not sustain their business and they also departed. Essential shops such as Royals' (grocers) Davis (newsagents), Brenda's (greengrocers) and 'June The Post Office' kept things going but eventually supermarket opposition and new technology won the day and they closed. It is impossible to believe that in 1879 Hotwell Road supported 194 shops and 32 pubs.

Local employment still centred on the harbour, but work dropped off when the wood yards closed on Cumberland Road, to be replaced by Baltic Wharf, a housing development. Across the float the area round Merchant's Dock became Rownham Mead and the sand and coal yard at Poole's Wharf became another attractive riverside estate. Fortunately these buildings were not allowed to be built high and as time passes and trees have grown, they have become part of the landscape.

The harbour seemed very empty when Campbell's Steamers left but there was still work available on the dredgers which left on most tides returning with sand scooped up from the Bristol Channel. This was off-loaded onto the dockside at Poole's Wharf before that was re-developed. This was home to the dredger 'Harry

Right: The 'Rose of Denmark' (bottom left) is completely dwarfed by the Flyover and new road system. The roads all go somewhere except one which is not needed. Can you identify it? The Piazza was noisy and very polluted and rejected by many local people.

ADGE CUTLER ON THE FLYOVER

The Bristol anthem, Virtute et Industrial and Back on the Farm were two songs written by Adge Cutler in 1967 that featured our beloved Flyover.

Here's a verse from the former and a still image from a music video about the latter showing Adge and his fellow Wurzels larking about on the Flyover.

With one way streets and flyovers
We knows which way we'em facing
Have you seen our brand new bridge?
Down at the Cumberland Basin?
The cars go by like thunder
Up and round and under
Just where they goes
No bugger knows
And t'aint no bleedin' wonder!

Brown', a familiar sight on the river, which was sold and sneaked away from Bristol on contract work in the Middle East. Once this was completed the boat was scuttled. If only Hotwells had known it would have given the 'Harry Brown' a truly great send-off. Fortunately, Fred Wedlock made a film about the boat for television. Now, only the MV Balmoral remains as a reminder of cruising days.

The other main employer at the time was W.D and H.O Wills where Florence Brown, first lady Lord Mayor of Bristol was a 'stripper'. Locals say the morning journey was like an army on the march as everyone queued up for the ferries at Mardyke and Gas Ferry Road, to cross the harbour to Bedminster and Southville. In 1974 a modern new factory was built at Hartcliffe and workers had to find their way out there on buses, bikes or... cars!

Some organisations were well established in the community. The Brownies met at Trinity Rooms as did the Skittles Club, but eventually that closed when plans were drawn up to alter Holy Trinity and create community space in the church itself. The Trinity Rooms became flats. Of course, people still had fun – a tug of war across the small inlet between the Nova Scotia and Dock Cottages would have been well worth watching, but the tennis courts by the Portway had gone and people no longer swam at Jacob's Wells Swimming Baths. Public amenities were disappearing fast in Hotwells.

Huge crowds turned out for events in the harbour. The launching of the Miranda Guinness, in 1976 the last boat built in Charles Hill's yard was very special, but nothing drew crowds like the spine-chilling powerboat racing. Harold Jarman, a Hotwellian, was the star of Bristol Rovers and Mike Rafter following in the steps of Sam Tucker played rugby for England. Enthusiasts discovered the challenge of rock climbing in the Gorge and were busy establishing new routes up the cliff face. Chris Bonnington (Everest) enjoyed the challenging climbs in the1970s and was last seen replacing tiles on a house roof on Hotwell Road – without a rope!

THE NEWCOMERS 1960 ONWARDS

All over the country a new generation was looking for work and somewhere to live. In the Hotwells/Cliftonwood area of Bristol they discovered run-down, semi-derelict buildings with obvious potential. The worst had been demolished during slum clearance, others not repaired after the war, but in some cases it was the problem of absentee landlords who could not afford to repair the properties and were willing to sell them cheaply just to get them off their hands. One house in Freeland Place was bought for £250 and Peter Ware, a charismatic local architect, bought a

Liz Marleyne in front of the house she bought in Hope Square in the 1970s after appeals against demolition were successful.

stunning corner house in Dowry Square for £200 including bed bugs! The 'newcomers' for that is what they were, made decisions that they would never regret. They bought the houses 'as seen' and it is no wonder that people who invested in the big lodging houses are regarded as the 'lucky generation' as they can now sell them for almost a million pounds (in 2020). People who bought the smaller Victorian and Edwardian houses, better suited to family

Cartoons by David Brown summing up DIY in the 1960s. Left: 'Mending a sash-cord - Madame Guillotine', Middle: 'Gulls on a roof', Right: 'Contemplation'

living, had less building work to do but have also profited. The same thing happened in many cities; new people bought houses and by improving them, increased the value. Local people who had lived in the same area for many years often chose to sell their property and move somewhere cheaper to enjoy the profits. Eventually areas became 'gentrified' and some that had been very rooted in community life changed accordingly. The community in Hotwells and Cliftonwood remained very strong at this time and although some local people moved away, most stayed. Asked what they thought of what had happened the local people said that, in hindsight, they wished they had had the sense to buy the houses and do them up themselves!

The 'Newcomers' of the 1950s and 1960s were not rich or wealthy and having scraped the money together, took a chance and bought houses badly in need of TLC. This involved a great deal of DIY which continued for many years. Some probably haven't finished yet! The new houseowners went on a steep learning course and achieved skills not taught in any school. Remember – there was no B&Q then, just the local hardware shop!

A 6-part BBC documentary series produced by John Boorman and Michael Croucher, 'The Newcomers' was broadcast in 1964 and featured the likes of Alison and Anthony Smith and Tom Stoppard among others about the young people who had moved into the area in the 1960s. It was also shown at The Watershed in a special screening in 2010.

Inevitably the local people were rather suspicious of their new neighbours but lasting friendships were soon made especially when help was needed with a blocked gully on the roof, or a gull's nest in a chimney. In a community like Hotwells there is always someone who can help or knows someone who knows someone who has got an extra-long ladder or a plunger.

During the 1970s, one event outshone all the rest. On Sunday July 5, 1970 the rusty hulk of the SS Great Britain was towed up the River. Enormous crowds lined

LETTER FROM PATRICK DROMGOOLE

Another local who appeared in one of the Newcomers episodes was Patrick Dromgoole, who wrote a letter about visitors to his home in Freeland Place during the 1960s:

"Thank you so much for your note. I did indeed pay £250 for that lovely house though three floors were let off and there was no bathroom. How marvellous that the rose still almost blooms in the ceiling. I spent a lot of time imitating Michelangelo working on that and Chalker sold it to you for £20,000; he did well – I think he paid me eight and now you are looking at £500-600k.

O'Toole spent quite a bit of time there, as did Richard Harris, Tom Stoppard, Charles Wood, Peter Nichols and John Boorman et al. I got married there, had all three of my children and then bought a derelict farm in Somerset and started again. Although brought up in London I've never been more than half urban, and now find Scotland's countryside a pretty good terminus.

Thanks for writing
Patrick Drongoole"

Return of the SS Great Britain to Bristol on July 5, 1970.

the bank at every vantage point, strangely moved at what they saw, but wondering what on earth would happen to it in the future. People had to use their imagination and the Council had to take major decisions to ensure the ship could be permanently berthed in its original dock as it interfered with road plans. What if they had said 'No'? As interest in the restoration grew it became obvious that although Bristol could never match Avonmouth for trading it offered the most incredible opportunities for leisure activities. The return of the SS Great Britain signified a whole new era for Bristol.

It was sad to note, however, that congregations at all the places of worship were dropping. The knock-on loss of income meant that it was increasingly difficult to raise funds to keep the buildings in good repair. Hope Chapel was in a bad way.

WANTED! SOMEWHERE WHERE THE COMMUNITY CAN MEET

The local people and the newcomers recognised that unfortunately, there was no place where a large number of people could meet up and get to know each other...

HOPE CHAPEL TO HOPE CENTRE

Work to convert Hope Chapel into a Community Centre well under way in 1977. The billboard is appealing for financial and volunteer help with the refurbishment. The conversion won an award from the Civic Society.

THE COMMUNITY FIGHTS BACK

The Community Association was formed in the early 1970s and Summer Street Fairs were organised which brought the whole community together. These were centred on Albemarle Row and the School Green. Stages were erected, groups performed and the event, which became very popular, was fuelled by cider. A great time was had by all! Albemarle Row was closed, traders set up stalls and tea and cakes were served in the School Hall.

Hotwells School had, without trying, become the centre of community activities and was being increasingly used by local organisations which rented the space. John Rees, Head Teacher and way ahead of his time, was very community minded and, had unbelievably, persuaded the Local Education Authority to let him employ a community teacher who worked both at the school and in the local area. Holiday Schools and After School Clubs were started, among the very first anywhere in the country. Use of the school premises threatened to escalate and thoughts turned to the derelict Hope Chapel across the hill at the end of Albemarle Row which was under threat of demolition. Mrs Stacey the school caretaker was one of the remaining members of the small church congregation which met in a room at the back.

The Congregational Federation had decided to apply for planning permission to demolish Hope Chapel. The Community Association stepped in and co-ordinated an application to restore Hope Chapel as a Community Centre. Once it was renovated and, in some parts, rebuilt, Hope Chapel became Hope Centre on a 20-year lease on the understanding that the small congregation could continue to meet on Sundays during that time. This they did until the group was disbanded in the late 1990s. The Chapel remained consecrated.

The team of volunteers including Peter Ware (Architect), Sue Otty, Janet Temple and Judy Williams.

Obviously, money had to be raised to fund the project and donations were received from many people, but it was the physical hard graft put in by individual volunteers that was most appreciated. The Community Association applied for and received a Manpower Services Grant which meant that work could begin. This project was overseen by Sue Otty who took on the unpaid responsibilities of seeing the job through.

Hope Chapel, now Hope Centre, opened its doors in January 1978 to serve the community in a totally different but equally caring way. Hope Centre was answerable to the Community Association who held the ultimate responsibility. What did the community want and expect? The popular Street Fairs were becoming too big and unmanageable, rather like early mini Glastonbury Festivals without free milk. The very last event of the last

Inside Hope Chapel in the early 1970s. The pulpit was stored in the School Room and disappeared when the building was demolished.

Street Fair was a gig by 'The Cortinas,' a group with local connections who played to a huge audience in the new venue. Nick Sheppard (later in The Clash) and Dan Swan, were offspring of two of the 'Newcomer' families.

The Centre was likened to a Village Hall – an amenity available for hire coupled with events being arranged for the community. All over the world people celebrate with music and dancing so the first event was a Ceilidh. The Grand Opening was eventually performed by Tony Hart of the BBC TV programme 'Take Hart'. This was an obvious choice as 'Morph,' star of the programme, was being produced by two young animators, Peter Lord and David Sproxton, (Aardman Animations) at Stork House on the Hotwell Road.

The Community Association had a venue where meetings could be held. It saw itself as the umbrella organisation bringing together, in an inclusive way, everything that was already happening in Hotwells and Cliftonwood. Trustees were appointed as was a Management Committee with Chairman, Secretary and Treasurer which planned and oversaw how the building would be maintained and run sustainably from day to day. Street wardens volunteered to keep everyone in touch. Helen and Ray Smith who conveniently lived nearby in the Polygon, became 'Keeper of the Keys,' but most essential of all a caretaker was employed to keep the place clean and tidy. Stella Pole and husband Dave, who became a well-known vicar and very popular on Radio Bristol took on the onerous job for a time. Gill Beedell became Housekeeper and established a Day Book which created a lively dialogue between Hope Centre and the users. Eventually Joe Sutton became the caretaker and did so for many years.

The Manpower Services Team had done a great job. Now the Centre had to be kitted out. Chairs and tables were installed, the kitchen revamped and Anthea Bruges obtained some rather spectacular gold coloured curtains of great length from a cinema in Weston-super-Mare to black out the big chapel windows. Pews still filled the far end of the gallery.

The Management team worked in the office at the top of the stairs. At first it was rather rashly decided that it could be the home of the Youth Club who, believing they could decorate without consultation, painted everything black with white graffiti 'decorations'. After repainting, the office moved in. Not an office by today's standards; there were no computers or internet, mobile phones or photocopiers at that time, but there was a typewriter, a telephone, a desk, several chairs and that's about all except that it was busy and welcoming. Downstairs, in the kitchen, the kettle was always on.

Plans for the building work including 'dream' plans for the conversion of the schoolroom which not only was based on a smaller chapel but had flats above designed to provide a sustainable income. Peter accepted no fees for his plans.

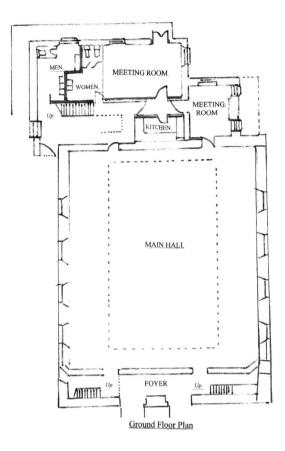

Ground Floor Plan

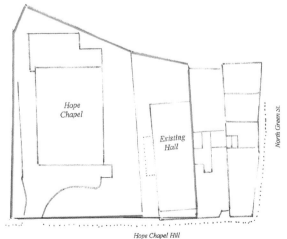

Hope Chapel Hill

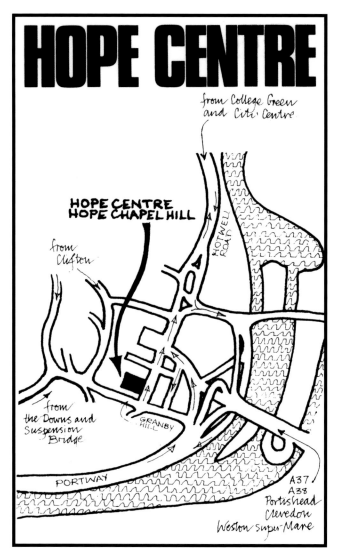

HOPE CENTRE

from College Green and City Centre

HOPE CENTRE
HOPE CHAPEL HILL

from Clifton

HOTWELL ROAD

from the Downs and Suspension Bridge

GRANBY HILL

PORTWAY

A37 A38
Portishead
Clevedon
Weston super Mare

How to find the Hope Centre as it appeared in the Sept-Dec 1983 'What's On Guide'.

In 1983 Sandra Fryer and Ray Smith co-ordinated a Community Programme using Government funding to provide 'Job Creation' for a team which at times numbered 18. They worked, many part-time, in the office, ran the kitchen, worked on improving play facilities in the school grounds, did gardening work, ran the Youth Club and generally enjoyed work experiences. As a result of this influx of people in the building, it became a very lively and busy place with Katherine Martin as Manager.

An old pew remains in Hope Chapel which became the star of the show when a group of the helpers, using ropes, hard hats and brute strength slowly lowered it from the balcony to the floor watched by a fascinated audience all holding their breath in case it fell. Thousands of people must have sat on it and it could tell quite a tale!

Activities were introduced for older residents as well as children and the Youth Club flourished. There was help and encouragement for people coping with a range of problems and disabilities achieved by bringing together local professionals, including social workers, the police, doctors and teachers who contributed some welcome 'joined up thinking'. For example, 'Our Chance', a group concerned with helping people with mental problems used Hope Centre as its base. Alcoholics Anonymous met regularly and there was help for those in debt. The then Member of Parliament held regular surgeries. At last, local people could be helped locally.

Eventually the Government scheme finished and it was decided to appoint a Hope Centre Manager. After Katherine Martin, four other women ran Hope Centre during its lifetime. Ros Robins, Dot Peryer, Ina Hume and Gill Loats all worked extremely hard and imaginatively, each contributing to Hope Centre's success in their own manner but inevitably, at the heart of their brief, was the need to raise enough money to keep the whole enterprise sustainable. Many volunteers were needed to help but such was the excitement at the start of the new venture it was not a big problem.

Groups renting the hall on a regular basis ensured a steady income, but it was also let out for parties and weddings. On one memorable occasion, caterers brought in portable ovens to heat up some lasagne but, quite unexpectedly, the door on one accidently flew open and the lasagne finished up on the floor. No problem. The delicious dish was served straight from the carpet and nobody ever knew – until now! The bar staff were once asked to slice up a wedding cake but the smooth white icing was rock hard and eventually a mallet, normally used for 'tapping a barrel' was employed to reveal the delicious cake beneath.

The bar proved to be a lucrative way of making money and over the years, it became very well run. Gillian Joseph had little idea of what she was taking on when she became the first chairman of the Bar Committee. There were two aims; to satisfy customers and make a profit. It all sounded easy but as there were no courses about running bars, everything was learnt through hard experience. It was very important for the programme of events to be finalised in good time to allow for licences to be applied for and granted. The bar was established in the kitchen but the beer was kept in a back room originally meant as a second meeting room. Smiles, the local brewer, delivered the beer and on one occasion when a ferocious thunderstorm was forecast they suggested cooling the barrels with wet blankets. One got an eiderdown! Dixie's produced the cider, the most popular brew being Cripple Cock. Spirits, wine and soft drinks had to be bought and collected from a wholesaler, but by far the most onerous job was arranging for volunteers to work on the bar and clear up afterwards. No wonder the late arrival of a dishwasher was greeted with cheers!

People got paid to work on special occasions, but all volunteers got free tickets for shows and gigs. Two bar helpers were sitting in the balcony enjoying a memorable presentation of 'The Mysteries', produced by Marion Reed when suddenly they found themselves in a spotlight and to their horror, God appeared in front of them on a fully extended fork-lift truck. Huge embarrassment! A Beer Festival failed to draw the expected crowds but someone got wind of the fact that a substantial amount of beer was

Douglas Merrit and Gareth Webb from one of the pantomimes showing the small kitchen/bar in the background.

left over, paid a visit and walked off with the lot!

The kitchen immediately became the 'centre of the centre' because everyone gravitated towards it, but it was never big enough. Staffed to feed employees as well as visitors it had many incarnations over the years and several different cooks provided wholesome meals, snacks and drinks. It was also available for visitors provided they brought their own milk and tea bags! At one point it became a serious café serving excellent meals of high quality, but the drawback was always finding somewhere to sit down especially if the meeting room was in use.

A Saturday morning visit to the Indoor Market, packed with rented stalls was both interesting, sociable and a way to help fund the Centre. It was an early start for the lads who set it all up and took it all down supervised by an efficient Les Agar. Alec Yirrell (Antiques Road Show)

COMMUNITY GROUPS WHO REGULARLY USED THE HOPE CENTRE

Youth Theatre • Welfare Advice • Yoga • Art for Everyone • Monday Club • Parents/carers and Toddlers • Children's Dance and Drama • Aerobics • Le Club Francais • Le Roc • Toy Library • Living Memories of Hotwells • Tap dancing • Karate • Rollerbooting • Baby Clinic • Latin American & Modern Ballroom • Free Legal Advice Surgery • Skittles • Indian Dance • Tea and Toast (Early morning club for mums) • Youth Club (Boys, girls and mixed) • Badminton • Music Workshop • 'Our Chance' • Roller Booting • Astrology • and many, many more.

A Saturday Market in the 1990s.

was usually among the first customers once he had helped his daughter set up her stall. He often struck lucky with a bargain. Regular stallholders sold a wide variety of goods from plants, cakes, bric-a-brac and vinyl records, to miscellanies of collectibles. It was a place to wander round, meet friends, spend money and have a drink at the bar. Just one problem. There was never room in the car park.

Jumble sales were great fundraisers but very hard work and there was always an indefinable smell that pervaded everything. A queue would form outside and once the door opened the customers would rush in and start turning over the piles of skirts, tatty shirts and shoes without laces searching for a bargain. On one occasion George Ferguson – former Bristol Mayor - bought some clothes which turned out to be his own, donated by his wife, earlier!

The New Year's Eve party was always a sell-out and crowds danced in the New Year to the music of 'The Old Fox' band and other lively groups. It took a great deal of organising but raised a lot of money. It was also good fun. Around 500 inflated balloons were strung across from one side of the gallery to the other to create the effect of a balloon ceiling which dropped on everyone at midnight. One minute's stamping and they had all gone! The children who were still awake absolutely loved it!

At Christmas many of the community united to sing carols and enjoy a mince pie. Music Workshop provided the music and the school joined in this Charity event. Kitsch Balls and Auctions were good fundraisers as well.

Programme from a performance of The Nativity by Hotwells Theatre Project 1986

HOPE CENTRE PROMOTIONS AND COMMUNITY ARTS

Almost as soon as Hope Centre opened a small group met with the Manager to compile a programme which complemented the regular programme of activities. Because it wanted to be entertaining, educational and inclusive, it proved very challenging and the group went on a steep learning curve. Basically, the programme included theatre or musical events at weekends but this varied. There was an agreement with the neighbours that 'noisy' music events would take place once a month and finish by 11pm so as not to disturb them.

What could Hope Centre offer to visiting performers? There was the big multi-purpose hall, but no stage. Black drapes could be hung from the balcony to provide an enclosed space for a performance area which could be lit by limited theatre lighting bought second hand. This needed to be fixed to a home-made scaffolding rig. The changing room was a small space behind the front doors but toilet facilities were available at the main entrance, reached by going outside and round the building. A quick dash if it was raining! Seating was put up and taken down for each performance. All this would appear to be very basic except that, almost without exception,

the performers loved coming to Hope Centre. Why? Because they felt free to use the space as they wanted and make it their own. Eventually Bristol City Council contributed towards the purchase of raked seating which replaced the rostra, made by volunteers, initially used to raise chairs for better viewing. It remains a miracle that nobody was seriously injured by falling off the seats. The raked seating was a great success and created a 'proper' theatre experience.

Joe Sutton, Jack of all trades, was caretaker at Hope Centre for many years, and a man who loved theatre. He was happiest sorting out leads, plugs and lights for a performance and was always fascinated to see how quickly a visiting company could put up a set. 'Crystal Theatre of the Saint' was the first company to use Hope Centre and in next to no time they transformed the hall into a fantasy wood. Joe was usually around when a company arrived and was always welcoming, showed them the kitchen and made them feel at home. He often helped with their lighting.

When Hope Centre eventually became Hope Chapel again a pile of posters was discovered. These, advertising many of the shows, performances and gigs that had

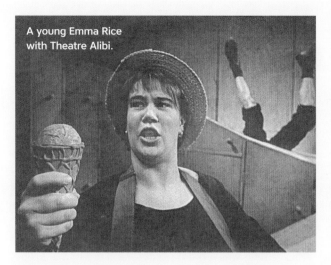

A young Emma Rice with Theatre Alibi.

Chorea Bohemica from Prague.

TOURING THEATRE COMPANIES WHICH VISITED HOPE CENTRE

Footsbarn • Public Parts • Innerroom Theatre Co. • The Rose Theatre Co. • Mr. Sands Theatre Co. • Riff Raff Theatre Co. • Theatre West • Trickster Theatre Co. • Natural Theatre Company • Avon Touring Theatre Co. • Desperate Men – Street Theatre • Cunning Stunts Theatre Co • Midstupidity Theatre Co. • Travelling Light Theatre Co. • Might And Main • Domestic And Industrial Theatre Co. • Belcikal • Orchard Theatre Co. • Cosmotheka • Women And Theatre Co • Theatre Alibi • Graeae • Bruhaha Theatre Co. • Talking Pictures • Acta Community Theatre • Strathcona Theatre • Green Ginger • Ridiculusmus • Anorak Of Fire • Rear Window Theatre Company • Temba • Age Exchange • Forkbeard Fantasy Theatre Co. • Bristol Old Vic Theatre School • Red Shift • Candoco • Theatre On A String • Remould • Covent Garden Comm. Theatre • Kneehigh • Hull Truck Theatre Co, • Taboo Theatre Co • Spare Tyre Theatre Co. • Tnt • Incubus Theatre Co. • Sensible Footware • Paupers Carnival Theatre • Solent People's Theatre Co. • Not The National Theatre • Commotion • Sedgemoor Theatre Co. • Nickelodeon • Les Bubb • Bare Bones Theatre Co • Scarlet Harlots • Medieval Players • Foolscap • Dr. Fosters • Mummerndada • Fusion And Kaboodle • And many others.

taken place were deposited at the University of Bristol's Theatre Collection which, in 2019, invited a group to go through them at a lunchtime get together. There was total amazement as the posters were spread over a large table. 'You never had them! How on earth did you afford it?' and 'I'll never forget them' and 'they were amazing' were among the comments overheard. The variety and quality of the performers was truly staggering. Nobody realised at the time how good so many of these companies and performers were or how famous some would become.

The 1970s, 80s and 90s was a rich time for small touring theatre companies who bombarded venues with publicity about their work. People visited Edinburgh Festival every year hoping to discover shows they thought the local audience would enjoy. Jenny Éclair made several appearances on their recommendation as did Medieval Players.

There was a commitment to support local companies. 'Travelling Light Theatre Company' and 'Gee Baby I love you' a popular local group, among them. Bim Mason who co-founded Circomedia and was connected with several other companies including 'Mummerndada' and 'Peepolykus' was a regular performer. 'Desperate Men', Britain's longest running Street Theatre Company, first appeared at Hope Centre and 'Avon Touring', based at the Albany Centre visited with their shows.

The initial grants received from South West Arts and Bristol City Council enabled a programme to be produced which matched the interests of the local audience but as time passed, despite the fact Hope Centre was once quoted as being 'The Jewel in South West Arts Crown', grants came with conditions attached which sometimes meant a performance might not cover its costs because it lacked local appeal. The Albany Centre, Van Dyck Theatre, (University of Bristol) and the Arnolfini, were all producing similar programmes at the time and, at one point, an alliance was formed. In order to save on publicity just one poster was produced with all the venues' planned events detailed on it.

Funding was a never-ending problem for everyone. Although grants were received from Bristol City Council and South West Arts they were only just sufficient and as there was no guaranteed funding for any length of time, forward programme planning was a nightmare. Artistes always received their contracted fee, but sometimes there was a box-office split between venue and performer or two venues got together and negotiated a 'bargain price' for a show at each venue. By far the best arrangement came with guarantees against loss. On top of this, 'sponsorship' became the buzz word and some money

came that way. Eventually the National Lottery helped. During Gill Loats' tenure as Manager, threatened cuts in funding by both Bristol City Council and the Arts Council led to strong protests.

Hospitality was often part of the deal for the visitors and a small blue book was kept detailing who was staying with who and when and for how long. The hosts were not paid but received complimentary tickets.

Publicity was everything. A programme was published three times a year together with a more local Newsletter both of which were initially delivered by hand! Eventually, standard sized programmes were printed, and Jeremy McNeil started an efficient business, driving round in his van delivering leaflets and topping up supplies. Some posters arrived from performers to be finished off in a blank space provided for the date, time, place and cost. After doing this arduous task, volunteers then trudged miles, persuading shopkeepers and pubs to display the posters. Before the internet, public notice boards were incredibly important and the sign of a lively community. Hotwells had none. Radio Bristol was always supportive as was the Bristol Evening Post, and Western Daily Press. Most important of all was 'Venue' which grew from 'Out West' that was the first magazine published with local listings. Shirley Brown, a local journalist, had undying support for Hope Centre and was very encouraging of theatre on local stages. She must have reviewed hundreds of shows, but was always positive and constructive in her comments. She bravely took a memorable part in one pantomime when, as a mermaid, she got completely drenched.

After several years, the theatre scene changed as people took courses in Theatre Management. It seemed sensible to hand over the work to a professional. Dot Peryer, who eventually moved on to manage the never boring 'Natural Theatre Company' from Bath, was the first to be asked to produce the Arts Programme but she also had to run the Centre and all the regular events as well.

GIGS AT HOPE CENTRE

Contributed by Gill Loats

I went to one of the first gigs at Hope Centre, **The Pop Group** 13th February 1979. Probably the one that forewarned the great and good of Hotwells that they perhaps had bitten off a little more than they could chew when it came to programming music. This very possibly led to the decree 'only one noisy per month'. By the time I arrived as manager in 1995 fear of punk had subsided but there was no shortage of local bands with at least 6 musicians and a horn section that could fill the brief for dancing and ensured a full house, a fruitful bar take and consequently, volume. The **'Losenges'** and **'The Soul Searchers'** had paved the way, and of course **'The Parole Brothers'** featuring local radio presenter **Keith Warmington (Will) Liam Henshall** before **Londonbeat** and neuroscience and fine guitarist **Steve Payne**. Steve together with **Chris Scott** were **Crawdaddy** who recorded an acoustic album called **Hope** at Hope Centre in 1998. Acoustic and not to be counted as far as I was concerned towards the 'noisy' rule are an example of some rule bending and a fuller music programme in the late 1990s as long as no one mentioned PA hire.

Bristol had long been reticent when it came to going out to see a band they hadn't heard of, so promoting bands on their way up was a gamble that saw some careful programming and mixed bag events like **Cabaret Esperanto**. **Henry Shafto**, local drummer, provided the idea and a resident band, to which we added music, poetry, circus and non-specific. Of course, Esperanto was spoken, but only by Henry. It was a lean time in Bristol for live music venues; obviously **The Fleece** kept going but many of our old haunts had been knocked down in the name of 'shopping mall 'progress. The DJ was rife and mega nightclubs were where young people went, so the Hope Centre was able to clean up in terms of names that 'had been' touring international artists and no-financial-risk benefits for good causes.

We were able to programme class acts, **Antonio Forcione**, **Matt Taylor**, **Boz Brosman**, guitarists that mattered. We revisited our pasts with **Peter Blegvad** of **Slapp Happy/Henry Cow** and **The Crazy World of ArthurBrown**. We had stomping good nights with local bands **The Crazy Bones, The Dukes** and New Years Eve with **Gee Baby I Love You**.

The **Tom Robinson Band** returned us to the 1970s and we invented karaoke waking the Polygon all singing **2-4-6-8 Motorway** and **Glad to be Gay**. We never really did the rock and roll thing but there were some truly amazing gigs and the venue is greatly missed.

It was demanding and a large amount of time was spent applying for grants some of which helped cover her own salary. Nevertheless, Dot hired a production of Kneehigh's 'Carmen' which took place at the ruined church in Castle Park. Amazing! All the managers took on board the new challenge but it was hard work.

Before a show the stage had to be set, seating arranged, and a volunteer would be in charge to ensure everything ran smoothly front of house. Volunteer bar staff would set up in the kitchen. It was then up to the performers to put on a show!

Of course, there were highlights and everyone has their favourites. Nobody will forget 'Cunning Stunts' and 'Scarlet Harlots' – both very entertaining women's groups. In one, a lady having previously warned everyone that she was almost nine months pregnant performed a very lively tap-dance. Everyone held their breath! 'Footsbarn' were a complete revelation and physically lived in Hope

Chris Bedell on the left as Master of Ceremonies and children performing 'Me and My Teddy Bear' in the production of Music Hall

Centre while performing stunning shows. Performances by 'Graeae' and 'Candoco' both performed by people with disabilities were inspirational. 'Kneehigh', a then unknown company outside Cornwall gave their first performance in Bristol at Hope Centre. The rest of their story is history.

An all-black male dance company 'Phoenix' received standing ovations but, quite unforgettable, was a visit by folk dance company, 'Chorea Bohemica' from Prague who, during a period when there was still an Iron Curtain, danced into everyone's hearts with a performance which should have been in a London Theatre. Afterwards, at a party given for them at Windsor Terrace, they again entertained their hosts and kept Hotwells awake well into the early hours. Nobody complained. They were that good! There were poets and comedians, comedies and dramas, puppets and poets. Nola Rae, mime artist, stunned everyone when, portraying Elizabeth I, she slowly, very slowly, disappeared into the back of a chair.

How did she do that?

A stilt walker juggling with fire from 'Medieval Players' burnt his hands and rushed into the kitchen to put them under the cold tap before returning to the hall as if nothing had happened. A producer once spent his time, not watching his company perform at all, but opened his heart to the bar staff as his wife had just left him!

For many years a gentleman turned up for performances but never appeared to have any money to pay for a seat. He was nick-named Mr Audience. He loved theatre and was knowledgeable about it so it was decided he could have a free seat. This went on for several years. Who was he and what happened to him?

Sadly, it was not possible to have a professional resident theatre company because regular bookings had to be honoured for the hall space. However, the local amateur company 'Crumbling Walls', so named because old walls are a continuing problem in Hotwells,

PERFORMERS AT HOPE CENTRE GIGS

Rodney Allen • The Losenges Cabaret Esperanto • The Coltraines • Bob Brozman • Hot Night From Tanzania • Kate Mcnab • Cindy Stratton • Sweet Soul Sisters • Contos Sul • Jake Peggs • Gee Baby I Love You • Parole Brothers • Skin The Peeler • Bill Smarme • The Hairy Marys • Ceile • Taboola Rasa • Happy End • Meet Your Feet • Three Caballeros • Coup D'etat And Jim Blowfield • Steve Payne And Sam Howard • Soundshapes • Blue Aeroplanes • Denise Black • Roaring Jelly • Losenges (Womad Benefit)) • Jo Swan Sextet • Good Old Buggers • John Stevens Quartet • Steve Mulligan Quartet • Samba Dukes • Ascension • Deshi Quartet • Toto La Mmposina • Klezmernauts • Acoustic Mania • The Technos • Womad Events • Sonic Tonic • Dukes And Crazy Bones • The Cortinas • Matt Taylor Blues • Back Room Band • Parole Brothers • Grupa Folia • Burach • Company Of Strangers • Waulk Elektrix • Alexander D Grant • The Ambling Band Alkasalsa • Cowdaddy Unplugged • Crazybones And Swamp Donkey • Pete Airey • Acoustic Blurt • Mind The Step • Brutal Folk Tradition • Bob Davenport And The Rakes • Keith Warmington • Bristol Jazz Reunion • Skikisha Drum And Dance • Deviant Mix • The Cowpokes • Martha Lewiss • Savourna Stevenson • Black Voices • Fantazia • Spiro • Also: Bristol Community Festival Benefits (The Moonflowers)

put on regular productions. Ray Smith and a willing team worked hard to get a high standard of performance which everyone enjoyed.

The never ending need for money meant that the community happily produced a whole range of one off events which brought people even closer together.

Music Halls were fun, attracting big audiences which enjoyed participation. A real Palace of Varieties! The band and choruses practised beforehand as did the children, but, because individuals performed party pieces or turns, some just turned up to perform on the night making it relatively easy to put together. The children sang 'Me and my Teddy Bear', endearingly and there was a traditional 'My Lords, Ladies and Jelly Spoons' Master of Ceremonies. Music Hall songs were sung with gusto and everyone greatly appreciated a performance of the 'Dance of the Little Swans' from 'Swan Lake' performed by Keith the Greengrocer with Tony (Baldrick) Robinson and others all wearing tutus. For some totally obscure reason a group of ladies dressed as angels once performed to the sound of electric hedge trimmers!

Meanwhile, Anne Jellico in Cornwall produced a challenging community play which started a fashion Hotwells could not ignore. Some places brought in professional companies from outside to help, but Hotwells decided to go it alone realising that part of the challenge could be to do it entirely without help. If mistakes were made, so what? At a brainstorming meeting it became apparent that there was an embarrassment of history to draw on and in the end three plays were performed over three successive years.

'The River' was first with John Turner commentating on the rules of the Harbour, followed by 'The Spa' in year two with the story of Lady Hope. The third was 'The Ups and Downs of Hotwells' including scenes from the Portway Tunnel during World War Two. Almost the same cast and group of children appeared in all three. These were not the huge, all-embracing plays that other places produced, rather three different performances each telling a different local story. The plays sold out and the profit was used to buy several much-needed notice boards for Hotwells.

Fred Wedlock brought an elderly lady with memories of Hotwells to one performance. She absolutely loved it but sadly died very soon afterwards. Fred assured us that 'she died happy!' He had once wanted a mortgage for a

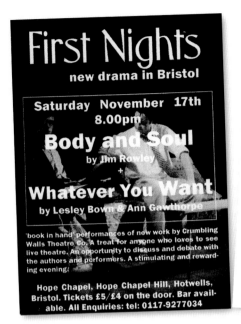
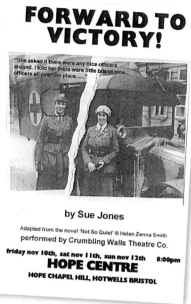
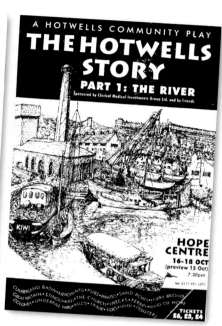

Crumbling Walls present both familiar plays and new writing. 'The Hotwells Story' was Part I of the Community plays.

house he fancied in Hotwells, but it was refused because the area was too run down at the time!

As Hotwells is a community of communities it seemed like a good idea if streets competed in a friendly way against each other at an evening entertainment. A number of streets took part most memorably Cornwallis Crescent who, in their performance, referred to the minutes of their Crescent Committee meetings and came up with a piece which continually returned to the subject of dog's mess. Unlikely people performed unlikely things and somewhere there is a silver plate which was awarded to the winner.

The Hotwells Circus was a mad, crazy show with clowns, Diana Wynne Jones and her totally untrained dog which failed to respond to any order she gave and Peter Ware who was shot from a cannon made of rusty dustbins jammed together. Peter, an architect who designed buildings for Bristol Zoo was impossible to direct and best left to do his own thing. Words cannot describe the different performances but Dennis Marks who became Director of the English National Opera in 1993, appeared as a lion tamer with a chorus line of lady lionesses. Tragically none of this was recorded on film.

Hotwells Carnival involved lots of children, workshops for making costumes etc, bands (The Ambling Band) and a procession round the community ending with a 'knees up' in Hope Centre. The school was very supportive and crowds turned out to watch the parade pass. Events such as these relied on Children's Scrapstore for materials to create extraordinary costumes and props made from the strangest of scraps. Scrapstore is like Ali Baba's cave – full of treasures!

CREATIVE WRITING

Creative writing is at the heart of any Community Arts Programme. Original work was shared at play readings, poetry recitals and of course, the Pantomime. Many writers from novelists, television scriptwriters, poets and writers for children live in the area, far too many to name, but journalists Helen Reid and Maurice Fells (both of whom worked for the local papers) have written many books about the area. Diana Wynne Jones, one of Britain's great writers for children, created wonderful fantasy books one of which, 'Howl's Moving Castle' was made into an animated film. Martin Parr has produced books of his idiosyncratic photographs to be enjoyed at the Martin Parr Foundation and Catherine Johnson has reached a worldwide audience after writing both the stage show and film 'Mama Mia.'

Back in 1993, Dot Peryer, then Manager of Hope Centre raised money to produce a book in just one week with contributions from 80 anonymous writers, many of whom had never tried to write creatively before.

Book Clubs flourished in the area but it was sad to see so many independent book shops close down in Bristol. Hotwells once had a fantastic Children's bookshop 'Where the Wild Things Are' but sadly that closed down when the owners moved away.

'Booksamazing', an event for Primary children, was held at Hope Centre for 14 years and attracted around 40,000 children. An annual event which brought together Hope Centre, The Puppet Place, Poetry Can, the School's Library Service and Bristol Old Vic Theatre School. It ran over two or three days presenting four sessions a day. The children enjoyed 'puppet telling' and poetry sessions exuberantly presented by students from the Bristol Old Vic Theatre School, before they were entertained by a celebrity writer. The first event was a huge Puffin Book Fair with Dick King-Smith, Michael Rosen and Diana Wynne Jones. Schools came from all parts and the whole event was inclusive. It cost just £1 per child and although funding initially came from Avon Local Education Authority, it was funded through sponsorship. There was a different theme each year from 'A Piratical Rumbustification' to 'The Body Show'. Some outstanding authors and poets turned up at Hope Centre including a young Ian McMillan (Poetry Please), Kit Wright (poet), John Ryan (Pugwash) and Dick King-Smith. Margo Price and Pauline Barnes helped at every performance and produced lunch when stimulating discussions took place between the young performers and the experienced writers. During all the performances only one little lad went to the loo! 'Booksamazing' only finished when the cost of transport to Hope Centre exceeded the £1 admission charge.

POETRY

There was always great support for local poets such as Libby Houston and Pat TV West as well as famous performance poets. Benjamin Zephania and the Liverpool Poets, Roger McGough, Adrian Henri and Brian Patten, all visited the latter presenting two shows in one evening. It was touch and go if the shows would break even. Thankfully there was a £12 profit! Ian McMillan was very popular but it was a performance of GRUTS by Ivor Cutler that few will forget. He asked that a harmonium be provided but the only one around had a

Illustration by Marc Vyvyan Jones.

LOSS LEADER
Poem written by Dick King-Smith for 'Booksamazing'

If you are English and indulge in sport
Then let this be your overriding thought
Regardless of the contest that you choose
You have to know the proper way to lose

Winning is easy. Any fool can shout
'Hurrah' and punch the air and leap about
Or fold his team mates in a wild embrace
Or spray champagne when he has won the race

But losing is a purely English art
No other country ever plays the part
As well as us. Not one of all the rest
Can match us in the way of giving best

Though we play up, play up and play the game
The net result is usually the same
That's not the point. Our great and native skill
Is losing well, while others lose so ill

Dick King-Smith signing autographs.

Whether it's billiards, badminton or bowls
Or making runs or scoring tries or goals
Whether it's Wembley, Wimbledon or what
There's one thing every English player's got

And that's the expertise of how to face
Defeat, and yet recite the saving grace –
'We didn't win? So what? Why make a fuss?
Nobody in the world can lose like us!'

missing B flat. He spent the evening playing round, and with, the missing note. He was quite extraordinary.

PUPPETRY
Puppetry was popular from the start at Hope Centre when a major event for children 'Bristol Puppet Theatre 84', part of the 'International Puppet Festival 1984' was presented. One of the benefits was the visit of Eric Bass, a puppeteer from the USA who performed his emotionally powerful show 'Autumn Portraits' to an adult audience. It was a tour de force. Jim Still and Di Steeds who founded

Puppet Van based at Art Space in Leonard Lane were taking puppets into schools and became involved. The children who visited were introduced to exciting forms of puppet telling, which were interactive and hands on. There was a performance at each session and Rod Burnett introduced his Punch and Judy show to the children but did not disclose how he used the swazzle. Julia and Anthony Row provided the marionettes.

Di Steed's puppets, created for

PUPPET THEATRE 84
A RARE PLEASURE

Joe Sutton with Marie Ware and Rod Burnett's sailor

Puppet Show outside the *Thekla* during the International Festival of the Sea in 1996. The two large seagulls also performed in the Hotwells Community Play that year.

the annual pantomime, were a high spot of every show whether it was an infestation of rats, a baby princess complete with pram (which subsequently appeared in the pantomime at Bath Theatre Royal) or a human chair (indescribable but wonderful!). Her puppets for Cabot Trip which was performed for the 'Festival of the Sea', outside the Thekla, included Arnold Fini, a merchant, and two enormous sea gulls which reappeared in the Community Plays.

Kate Pollard managed Puppet Place for several years, some of it from a cupboard office in Hope Centre where Rachel McNally worked as a volunteer. Rachel became administrator for the Puppet Place in their home on Harbourside where it has become one of the foremost puppet organisations in the country.

Dave Sproxton and Peter Lord visited Hope Centre to work with children at the time they were making Morph in Stork House. Meanwhile, over the road, in a unit under the Flyover, the Bolex Brothers were producing animated films, the best known being 'The Alternative Tom Thumb' and the film of 'The Modern Magic Roundabout.'

Jason Hill made a good link between professional and community arts when money was secured to present an early animation project with Aardman Animations.

THE VISUAL ARTS

Bristol City Art Gallery holds wonderful collections of paintings by Samuel Jackson and Rolinda Sharples both of whom lived in Hotwells during the 19th century and produced work which not only gives aesthetic pleasure but information about Victorian Hotwells. The Gorge and River Avon were favourite subjects as was Brunel's iconic Suspension Bridge and of course, the harbour always provides a rich source of inspiration. Hope Centre introduced a small gallery (in the gallery) but it was very vulnerable. It was, however, decided to mount an exhibition at the Create Centre Gallery entitled 'Art from the Heart of Bristol'. Many talented practising local artists were represented including Robert Hurdle, Peter Swan and Trevor Haddrell. Richard Long RA turned up on his bicycle with a sculpture which immediately raised the cost of the insurance! Denny Long who ran a Saturday Art Club for children at Hotwells Primary School displayed work as did Joanna Wright, John Stops, Rachel Hemming-Bray and Ros Grimshaw who made the wonderful Creation Window for Chester Cathedral in her studio at Windsor Terrace. There were many others and photographer Martin Parr gave a sell-out talk. 'Art on the Railings' extended the event to a wider range of artists both professional and amateur and a different audience. Large banners decorated Albemarle Row. The event was funded with a grant from the National Lottery who made a film about the exhibition to encourage other communities to do similar events and apply for small grants.

'Hats off to Brunel' part of City-wide celebrations of the great man's achievements was also held at the Create Centre. David Thornley (potter) made umpteen miniature pottery Brunel hat egg-cups and a group of children made pin-hole cameras. Local artists displayed pictures round the Brunel/Hotwells theme and a competition for the best model showing an alternative use for Brunel's famous hat was won by Clark's Pies of Southville who turned the hat into a pie oven! All exhibitions could have taken place at Hope Centre were it not for the regular, ongoing bookings by local groups. It was some time before Arts Trails were

ART FROM THE HEART OF HOT WELLS ART FROM THE HE ART OF HOTW ELLS **ART FROM THE HEART**

introduced which introduced the work of many more artists to a wider audience.

LIVING MEMORIES OF HOTWELLS

Lynda Stahl and Helen Smith originally brought older residents together to talk about and share memories of Hotwells and Cliftonwood. A regular group, eventually run by Margo Price, continued to do so and still meets regularly at Holy Trinity (2020). It is always a convivial evening but there are still very strong opinions about the deal they were dealt when the Flyover was built. It destroyed part of their lives as they lost friends they had known for years when houses were demolished. They regard the car as having destroyed any hope of the Hotwell Road ever serving the community as they remember it and they loathe the fact that as they get older, life becomes more difficult as there are so few local services.

Nevertheless, it was their help that made the 'Millennium Photographic Exhibition' worthwhile. It was

Margo Price with the Living Memories Project.

HOTWELLS MUSIC WORKSHOP

Contributed by David Burns

Trying to pin down what makes a community 'special' is never easy – but Hotwells Music Workshop must feature for hundreds of people. I, for one, would never have taken up the bassoon in my late thirties had I not had Music Workshop on my doorstep, and there are many others whose lives have been similarly enriched as they grew from adult beginner at Music Workshop to fairly competent player. This, in turn, feeds amateur orchestras and spin-off groups playing at home - all of which is fun, but also plays a serious role in strengthening the city's cultural fabric. Likewise, a high proportion of those signing on for the first time describe themselves as 'rusty': after all, life gets complicated as families, careers and the rest begin to impinge – and suddenly the once-competent flautist finds it's nearly twenty years since she played! But, with a format that only requires a six-week commitment, it's hardly surprising that Music Workshop appeals to busy people.

It all began in 1971 when Edward Williams (professional composer – remember 'Life on Earth?) and wife Judy were parents at Hotwells Primary School. Seeking to encourage amateur music-making and support music at the school, they came up with an idea for a PTA activity promoting instrumental chamber music and a choir. The school year was divided into six six-weekly sessions and people encouraged to sign up for one session at a time. The players were then put into viable chamber groups by the organiser and music selected from the extensive library which currently has around 1,300 works. Each session consisted of five rehearsal weeks and a concluding in-house concert at

Edward Williams, composer who, with wife Judy, started 'Music Workshop'.

which each group played its allocated piece to the rest. The pattern then repeated for those who chose to sign on again, but with different music and personnel. Thus, a clarinettist able to commit to the first three sessions of the year might have six weeks working on a Mozart trio, six weeks on a modern piece for four clarinets and then six weeks on a baroque quintet for mixed wind and strings.

Open to all comers (other than those with very little previous experience), there were no rules, no committee, no external coaching: this was to be a self-help co-operative in which beginners and the less experienced might well find themselves playing with and learning from other very skilled players. The format was inspired, with its variety of music, personnel and musical challenge – with the result that Hotwells Primary School has resounded to amateur music-making on 36 Thursday nights per year for the past 48 years thanks to the persistence of the six volunteers who took over the organisation from the Williamses. Numbers ebb and flow, of course – but each session attracts between 25 – 40 people. Astonishingly, not a single session has had to be cancelled, though the odd Thursday here and there may have been lost to snow.

Whilst it started life as a PTA activity, Music Workshop soon began to attract people from the wider community and beyond. A couple of copycat workshops started up elsewhere in the city and Thursday-night bar takings at local pubs benefitted. That said, the organisers have consistently worked to keep the various spin-off events school and community focussed. At school carol concerts we've paired-up with children learning instruments; we've provided the basis of an orchestra (and conductors) for community carol concerts; we've commissioned works from local composers – including one piece which included a poem written and sung by children from the school; we've given demonstrations at school Music Weeks; we've helped with the funding of school pianos and music stands ... And for nigh-on 2,000 Thursday nights, four different Headteachers and their tolerant staffs have trustingly given the run of the entire school

to a total of what must be close to 60,000 people!

Hotwells Music Workshop was – and remains – a striking innovative concept which has had a real impact on the lives of individuals and the musical life of the community. For Edward it was 'a place where we can all improve our musical skill and experience through a process of self-help and mutual support, each gaining and giving what they can. Whilst we aim to sing/play as well as we can, we share the view that music-making is principally a pleasurable social activity where our skills can develop in a relaxed, supportive setting'

their photographs, memories and enthusiasm that meant a collection of hundreds of pictures, now belongs to the community. Original photographs were borrowed, photocopied and returned, but every image was enlarged to A4 making it much easier to see the detail. Sometimes the story lies in the background. A £2,000 National Lottery award made the event possible. A request for pictures by David Harrison in the Evening Post and one by Keith Warmington on Radio Bristol opened the floodgates and although warned that there could be a poor response, nothing could have been further from the truth. Audrey Havens rang within minutes of hearing Keith and told the story of how her husband, then aged 16 had captained the John King Tug after the war simply because there was nobody else to do it. Then the pictures started arriving with fascinating stories, from people who had worked on Campbell's steamers or the ferries to a man who fished dead bodies (mostly cows/sheep) from the river. There were sad stories such as how Captain Livingstone one of Campbell's captains, lost his small son in Cumberland Basin and happy ones when crowds on the riverbank watched the motorboats racing to Portishead for the Fedden Trophy. (Nobody knows where that is!) Every

picture tells a story!

A fabulous photograph album created by Mr Hardy during the early part of last century tells the story of life in Cliftonwood and the area at the bottom of Jacob's Wells. This was very exciting and a real 'find'.

Radio Bristol focussed on local history as the Millennium approached and Hotwells and Cliftonwood were well represented in an exhibition they organised at what was then The Council House.

The Hotwells and Cliftonwood history display at the Radio Bristol exhibition in the late 1990s.

SPORT AND KEEPING FIT

Badminton started almost as soon as the lines had been painted on the floor of Hope Centre. Basketball was also available as was the skittle alley, but it was the yoga classes, aerobics and keep fit groups that were most popular.

It was not unusual to see bikes parked up outside the building and cycling was always encouraged. An annual bike ride from Hope Centre followed different routes for different abilities. 'Cyclebag' was the first cycling organisation in Bristol leading to a Sustrans campaign led by John Grimshaw, which successfully campaigned for a cycle network across the country. A ceramic map is displayed outside 'We the Curious' in Bristol made by Sue Ford and Marian Tucker to celebrate its success. Although crowds cheer on the cyclists in the big events along the Hotwell Road, local cyclists know that the greatest local achievement is to get to the top of Granby Hill, Constitution Hill or Clifton Vale without getting off to push.

Nowadays people can learn to sail, row and enjoy water sports in the Harbour but it is only recently that the water condition has improved. In the 1950s local children skinny dipped in the 'muddy' Merchant's dock. On one occasion a group were seen by the local policeman who chased one lad, right along the Hotwell Road. It raised a laugh as the guilty boy did not have time to get his clothes on! Sadly, a number of children were drowned when messing around in the docks, and Mr Berman gave money for Hotwells Primary School to build a learner pool on their premises. Jacob's Wells swimming pool was brilliant for a swim but it also served as a bath in the early 1900s with running hot water. Many people used this facility including the boys from the Industrial School overlooking Mardyke.

Sam Tucker (1895-1973) played rugby for England as did Mike Rafter. Harold Jarman played football for Bristol Rovers but after a match always asked 'How did City do?' Mark Dudbridge, son of Keith and Brenda who ran the greengrocers on the Hotwell Road throws darts at a professional standard not usual at the local pubs.

Nobody will forget the first time the hot air balloons flew in Bristol and regularly give everyone a free show. For local people there is always the feeling that a balloon might actually land on their house or in the garden. Now that would be something to talk about! One or two dipped in the river and one balloonist daringly went under the bridge early one morning watched by spectators on the Portway wearing pyjamas and eating toast.

Air balloons in the Avon Gorge.

BACK TO HOPE CHAPEL AGAIN

owards the end of the 1990s a report was produced with plans for the future of Hope Centre. Annie Scott, architect drew up exciting designs which would provide the Centre with more facilities such as spaces where people could hold meetings. There was also an intention to refurbish the building and take it into the 21st century.

Negotiations opened with the Congregational Federation as the original 20 year lease had run out. As before, the Community Association offered to allow worship by a Christian Group on Sundays. Negotiations were almost completed when the Federation was approached by Silas and Annie Crawley from Christchurch, Clifton, who persuaded the Federation to allow them to take over Hope Centre as a place of worship. This was agreed and Hope Centre handed the building over.

It all came as a terrible shock but it would be wrong to dwell on it. Maybe Hope Centre had had its moment in time and there is no doubt that in today's climate, funding activities would be an entirely different scenario. Parking would have become impossible for the numbers attending events. The Tobacco Factory in Southville now does much the same job, but sadly cannot provide the day-to-day community activities that Hope Centre offered.

Nonetheless, the 20 years of Hope Centre were exciting and fulfilling and many thousands of people benefitted. Hope Chapel did all the necessary building work much of it to the ideas put forward by Annie Scott. It is very much the same and still well used. A beautiful crypt has been constructed beneath the Chapel which can be let.

The community wish Hope Chapel every success and of course local people are delighted and relieved that the Pantomime is still seen as an important annual event in the community calendar and hope this continues for as long as so many people want it.

And now, as they say in the trade, it's time for something completely different!

AND NOW FOR SOMETHING COMPLETELY DIFFERENT!

It fits - the first pantomime in Hotwells. The first 'Cinderella' at Hotwells National School in 1948 with Jeanette Beacham, Diana Whitlock, Ann Moss, Joan Davis, Valerie Wise, Sheila Tubey and Carole Roach.

PANTOMIME HOTWELLS STYLE

A **visit to a pantomime is traditionally a Christmas treat.** In Hotwells, performers in the 40 year-old Pantomime tread the boards in early March. Why? Because the pantomime keeps people cheerful and busy during the depressing days of January and February. It is very important that everyone involved enjoys the experience and if an audience pays to see a performance so much the better as it raises money to spend on community projects. There is a Committee which oversees everything and gives grants to good causes such as the Lunch Club at Holy Trinity, or the Piazza.

It all started with a revue memorable for the performance of a shadow show performed by Brian and Margo Price. Nobody watching had the least idea of what was going on, let alone the performers but it was hilarious, and the audience loved it. The whole event was judged a success and the group decided to go one better than a revue and try pantomime.

The first attempt was 'Cinderella' in 1981 with Debbie Cranston as Cinders, Bill from the Bookshop was Buttons and a young George Ferguson was King with a crown decorated with wobbly balls. The musical choruses held it all together. The only scenery was a fireplace which hung precariously from the gallery together with black curtain material bought at the Market which enclosed the 'stage' area. That was fine when lit from the front, but when those lights were out and lights were on behind the curtains it was possible to see shadows of people moving around, some getting changed! It got the best laugh of the evening!

There was a chorus of punks and Cinderella went off to the ball in a trailer behind a bicycle. However, a serious problem became apparent. There was little continuity

Debbie Cranston, the first Hope Centre 'Cinderella' in 1981

Janet Temple looking for her horse.

Stephen Wickham with a new Princess.

between scenes and as each was written and produced by a different person it was like watching eight different plays. Fortunately, 'Cinderella' was a well-known story and the puzzled audience seemed to know what was happening. This situation continued for a couple of years until everything was pulled together, edited ruthlessly and someone put in charge. Amanda Webb and Sue Stops took on the joint job of holding things together which they did for many years until Gill Loats took over as Director

and Amanda as Producer. The show takes place over four days at Hope Centre and fortunately the congregation at Hope Chapel still allow it to happen and hopefully enjoy it!

PRODUCTION AND DIRECTION

These people hold the pantomime together. The Producer has to know everything that is going on and sort out any problems that might occur. This is not an easy job at times but very satisfying, as is that of directing the

Children enjoying one of the choruses.

show. The director brings discipline, common sense and imagination and is indispensable. The Musical director is equally important.

THE SCRIPT

Pantomime traditions are worth sticking to. The 'goodie' comes in from stage right and the 'baddie' from the left. The Dame is played sympathetically, but amusingly, by a man dressed as a woman who holds the whole thing together. The Principal Boy is played by a youngish thigh-slapping female who falls in love with a demure, sweet young girl. All this must be mighty confusing for the 30 or so primary school children sitting on mats in front of the action, waiting to do their bit, but they accept it all without question. By the end of the run they know all the words and sing the songs but only mouth the love songs. Bless!

Although most pantomimes have followed a

The Band looking more like an Orchestra. Left to Right: Nicky Claxton, David Nash, Lavinia Ferguson, James Bruges, Katherine Martin, Norman Golding, Sue Otty, Julian Dale and Kay Thomas.

traditional path, new ideas are always welcome and offer interesting creative opportunities. Up to a dozen would-be writers meet up in October to choose and plot the show which usually follows the traditional path with some pretty extraordinary deviations. Basically, a well-known fairy/pantomime story is manipulated to make it unique to 'Hotwellia'. Each writer, or group, produce a scene and returns with it to a later meeting to be read through. This ensures that continuity is established, and characters developed. Finally, the script is sent to the editors who are ruthless. Sometimes a whole scene might be thrown out or re-written, to ensure a slick panto! Everything gets printed before the read-through which takes place just after Christmas. Nothing is supposed to be changed after that, but of course, it is. After a read-through of the script, potential performers write the part they fancy playing on a piece of paper after which the writers endeavour to match a part to a person.

Anyone from the local area is welcome to take part and newcomers are always welcome. There are no stars, prima donnas or auditions. Ages range from five to 80-ish, so it is most definitely inclusive! Taking part is not exclusively acting, singing and dancing, it could be back stage work, scenery painting or helping with costumes and props. Most important of course is the music and the 'real' band which, in many different incarnations, has attracted a loyal following. Every contribution is appreciated.

Originally, rehearsals were held in the Meeting Room and the foyer at Hope Centre. However, it was cramped and cold and eventually there was a move to the more spacious Holy Trinity. The Adam and Eve, Rose of Denmark or the Merchant's Arms, were where the first programmes were devised and performances analysed. It was soon apparent that audiences enjoyed things most when something went wrong. Perhaps a piece of scenery collapsed, somebody forget to come on at the right time or a wig or moustache fell off. Unfortunately these events cannot be repeated.

Useful hints are offered to actors. The first is not to ad-lib as other actors rely on cues. The second is to try not to 'corpse' or start laughing. Yes, this makes the audience laugh but the show loses continuity which can be hard to pick up. The third is not to have a drink before the show as this leads to lack of concentration. The cast tend to ignore all this good advice! The show is rehearsed for just two hours a week at the Trinity Rooms starting at 8pm and stopping promptly at 10pm so people can get to the pub. Half the show is practised one week and half the next which does not add up to a lot of rehearsals but focusses the mind wonderfully. The total rehearsal time is about 24 hours although some actors like to rehearse 'special bits' privately. Ideally the cast should know their words by week three. They do nowadays, but at the beginning some never bothered to learn them until the very last moment.

MUSIC

Music is everything in the pantomime. Sue Otty, who plays the piano, persuades her musical friends to perform in the band for four nights. She then arranges and writes for clarinet, flute, trumpet, (Norman Golding was a Lord Mayor's Trumpeter) cellos, violins, drums and sound effects. It takes ages and she has done it for 40 years!

The band rehearses separately then turns up at the dress rehearsal where they have their own position in the hall. From there Sue Otty can keep her eye on just about everything and can prompt if necessary. The brilliant band is a luxury not enjoyed by many big pantomime productions where electronic music is often used. The audience is treated to songs with specially written Hotwell Panto words sometimes, displayed to enable the audience to join in. Loudly! Everyone joins in the rousing opening chorus to get the show off to a good start and again in the finale to celebrate a satisfactory conclusion. Tuesday night rehearsals start with everyone practising the choruses when Sue Otty sometimes rants and raves in order to get things up to scratch. For many, her performance is the high spot of the evening. A 'ting' song is written for the young lovers.

Meanwhile, the children and teenagers practice once a week. There are just two rehearsals when everyone gets together at Hope Chapel, the second of these being the dress rehearsal. Whichever way you choose to look at it, it should not work, but miraculously, it does.

COSTUMES AND MAKE UP

What to wear? This is by far the most exciting and entertaining part of the pantomime for most people. Initially everyone provided their own costume for the early shows with some only appearing at the first performance. Margo Price was a bug in a scene based on 'The Ugly Bug Ball' but nobody had seen her costume and nobody recognised the bubble-wrapped person with joke shop eyes on springs, who appeared just minutes before she was due on stage. It was brilliant but a tremendous shock to the children she was performing with especially when the bubble-wrap started to come apart! The women's chorus performed the Frog's Chorus in 'Sleeping Beauty'. Diana Moran, TVs Green Goddess kindly lent the ladies some of the green elasticated leotards that she was famous for wearing. Diana was slim and beautiful and

Margo Price as an Ugly Bug.   Ian Duncan and Carole Gough.   Alastair Sawday with 'The Wig'.

inevitably some of the leotards were put under great strain. There were, to be honest, significant bulges, but nobody cared because the audience cried laughing! They looked fantastic and the chorus line was born.

Nowadays the men enjoy chorus work as policemen, cooks or crooks, cyclists, pirates or Vikings, you name it. Of course, anyone can choose to be in any of the choruses but Ros Bennett has always appeared in the men's chorus and it wouldn't look right without her. She is small and the men are mostly tall and macho, but she always manages to steal the show. The rest of the cast get more inventive every year. From rats to judges, Onion Johnnies or mermaids to Knights in Armour, the costumes get better and better. Many people help sew them but most are still home-made and paid for by the wearer. They remain in cupboards, moth-infested lofts and garden

sheds to remind the owner of their 'moment of glory'.

A costume enables an actor to relate more easily to the character they are portraying and the same goes for makeup. Paul Crossthwaite is particularly remembered for the Rice Krispies stuck to his face to look like some horrible pox. A great 'ugh' went up from the audience when he picked one off his face and ate it. Then everyone laughed. Make up has completely changed since the greasy stuff used in the first pantos. Face paints are brilliant. Wigs, too, are now cheap and fun and without doubt the pantomime helps keep the joke shops in business. Pan Radford has changed many faces!

Just one outfit is special. Bristol Old Vic were clearing out some unwanted costumes and offered them to the Pantomime in return for the laughs they had had. Many students came to see how not to do it! Among them was a costume fit for a King which gets used every time there is a Royal personage. Eventually, all the costumes except the King's went to the Theatre School for recycling!

SCENERY AND PROPS

There is not a lot of room backstage so the job of stage manager is essential. Everything has to be in the right place and everyone has to know what they have to do. The first scenery was almost non-existent simply because no-one had the skills to produce it, but once a group emerged there was no stopping them. Scenery sets a story in time and place but in the restricted stage area at Hope Chapel where there is no stage or a proper front curtain, there is a great need for ingenuity and creativity. A large mat now covers the badminton court markings which were quite distracting during the early days. One expected a shuttlecock to suddenly fly in stage left. The mat also deadens the noise of shoes clonking around. There is nothing more distracting that the Principal Boy in high stiletto-heeled boots striding noisily across the stage to sing a love duet.

Janet Magrie arrived and took designing the set very seriously. She made small models to work from and must, with many other helpers, have painted acres of scenery. This became easier when large boards were made which could be bolted together to make a flat surface rather than drapes to be painted on. There have been stately home sets, gardens, rough seas, prisons, banqueting halls and kitchens. There are no fly facilities in Hope Centre although some scenery is hung down from the balcony. This demands special skills from the scene-shifters but it is the most likely cause of laughter if it goes wrong.

The scenery is painted in a barn somewhere deep in the countryside. As this happens in January and February stalwarts wearing innovative warm, paint-proof clothing are the unsung heroes of the pantomime.

There is no end to the inventiveness of the prop makers be it mechanical engines such as pie making

In days of old when knights were bold.

A sausage machine.

machines, to geese, golden eggs or hobby horses. The cast often make their own, but Di Steeds' puppets and bigger items made by Lynda Hunter, David Brown, Henry Acland and Paul Crossthwaite are always admired and appreciated.

The backstage and gallery teams under the supervision of the Stage Manager, work in cramped, dark conditions. It all has to be well organised and co-ordinated.

Janet Margrie in front of one of her sets.

LIGHTING AND FILMING

The initial lighting came from a few second-hand theatre lanterns bought with money raised at a benefit gig by Chris Harris who bravely sat through every pantomime. Unfortunately they could not produce the bright 'Strictly Come Dancing' lighting needed to create an exciting atmosphere, so spotlights hand-operated from the Gallery were hired in to do the trick. However, subtle use of lights can create atmosphere as in dark dungeons, a storm or a haunted house. In early pantomimes a scene lit by ultra violet light, was performed by the children who made fish, stars or planets, set in underwater or sky scenes, from cardboard shapes painted with fluorescent paint. Smoke machines are used sparingly as the hall quickly fills with smoke, nobody can see what is going on and the audience coughs. Pyrotechnically nothing can equal the colossal bang created when Peter Ware was shot from a cannon.

Steve Stunt (retired HTV cameraman) has filmed most of the pantomimes, some on videos but now on DVDs. Steve records the whole show then edits it to make it more fun. On one occasion he filmed the men's chorus dressed as knights, visiting the pubs at Cumberland Basin! They were supposed to look drunk, and probably were! The DVD is given a special showing for everyone involved.

Many people help put the show on the road from the person who fixes the dates of performances and rehearsals to the people who produce the programmes. These used to be A4 folded and somehow all the information was squeezed onto one sheet of paper. Nowadays a novel, imaginative programme is produced which raises the profile of the show. Tickets are printed and sold professionally, and publicity in local papers and on the internet is organised. Front of House deals with the needs of the audience on the night.

SHOW TIME

On the day of the show the hall must be prepared. The stage mat goes down on the floor and the scenery erected. The rake of seating is pulled out from its home against the back wall, an event well worth watching as it is noisy and needs brute force to pull it into position. There is room for about a hundred people who have to sit pretty close to each other if everyone is to get in. The seats are bench-like comfortable and none are reserved. As the tickets usually sell out a queue waits for returns but nobody has ever been turned away although they might not have seen much!

Attendants in purple and yellow 'IT'S BEHIND YOU!'

LIST OF PANTOS

Cinderella	1981 (1992, 2005)
Babes in the wood (with Robin Hood)	
	1982 (1995, 2009)
Dick Whittington	1983 (1993, 2006, 2018)
Aladdin	1984 (1997, 2016)
Jack and the beanstalk	1985 (1994, 2010)
Sleeping beauty	1986 (1996, 2007)
Puss in boots	1987 (1999)
Snow White	1988 (1998, 2008, 2017)
12 Dancing Princesses	1989 (2001, 2015)
Treasure Island	1990 (2000, 2011)
Sinbad	1991
Cinderella	1992
Dick Whittington	1993
Jack and the beanstalk	1994
Babes in the wood	1995
Sleeping beauty	1996
Aladdin	1997
Snow white	1998
Puss in boots	1999

Treasure Island	2000
12 Dancing Princesses	2001
Mother Goose	2002 (2019)
Beauty and the beast	2003 (2014)
Princess and the pea	2004
Cinderella	2005
Dick Whittington	2006
Sleeping Beauty	2007
Snow White	2008
Robin Hood (with babes in the wood)	2009
Jack and the beanstalk	2010
Treasure Island	2011
Ali Baba and the 40 Thieves	2012
King Arthur and the knights of the CB	2013
Dr Frankenstein meets Beauty and the beast	2014
12 Dancing Princesses	2015
Aladdin	2016
Snow White	2017
Dick Whittington	2018
Mother Goose	2019
The Mardyke Mermaid	2020

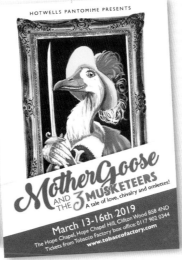
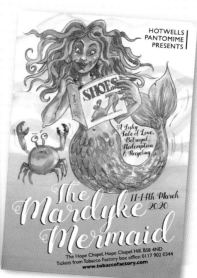

Ray Smith in the 'Kings' costume.

The Happy Couple.

Kate McNab.

shirts make sure everyone is comfortable. A countdown starts as the clock reaches seven and right on the dot, the audience is let in. There is a rush for the seats and by 7.15pm the hall is almost full. The atmosphere is warm, welcoming, and noisy as friends meet up, some having travelled miles to see the show. The children are already sitting on mats at the front, packed snacks at the ready for the interval. Mary, the chaperone gives them last minute instructions. Ices in the freezer are checked. The orchestra tunes up.

Backstage there is an air of excitement and dry-mouth fear. People are studying scripts to check on cues, strutting round in costumes looking for a long mirror. Praying. Fear is the great motivator. The fear of making yourself look a fool in front of family and friends.

Some last minute instructions from the Producer who wishes everyone 'Good Luck.' The lights go down and the overture starts.

Excited applause follows the overture and then... it's SHOW TIME!

The nine scenes should flow like clockwork with an interval after Scene Five when people descend on the Bar for refreshment and the children eat their snacks or an ice-cream. They will have already performed once and will do so again in the second half which starts with the teenagers who surprisingly, don't seem to mind performing with small children and OAPs one little bit. There is a lot of shouting out by the audience who enjoy any chance to participate.

There have been some pretty memorable scenes in the past. The most unforgettable was when a fountain was created by women resembling statues. The Trevi Fountain in Rome was the obvious inspiration. Large quantities of water was poured over the human statues

Margo and Brian Price in an early flan flinging scene.

down to two silver mermaids, complete with tails, who sat at the foot. Everyone got soaked and the audience had laundry problems.

In no time at all it is all over. The sleepy children go home. The cast can't believe that they have actually 'done it' and they head for the pub to celebrate. Hopefully the audience have enjoyed it and go home happy.

On the last night everything is cleared up so that Hope Chapel can start functioning normally again next day. It takes just over an hour to return the hall to normal the biggest job being to push the rake back against the wall and dismantling the scenery. Then, it's as if absolutely nothing had happened! Party time follows in somebody's house to celebrate another Hotwells Pantomime and thank all those who have been involved. The total number is always well over one hundred.

It is more than 300 years since Hotwells enjoyed the 'pantomime' of the Spa. For 40 years the local community has enjoyed itself and celebrated with a traditional pantomime. The continued pleasure enjoyed by so many should secure its future.

We queued to see the panto,
We queued to get some booze,
We queued to get an ice cream,
and then to use the loos.

We queued to leave the theatre,
We queued to get the bus,
The actors missed their cues all night,
But did we make a fuss?

Top left: The Fountain scene when people got very wet.

Top right: Gill Loats, Sue Stops, Nicola Crosse and Amanda Webb 3x Directors and the Producer.

Bottom: The Cast of Mother Goose and the Three Musketeers in 2019.

If you are feeling miffed that you haven't been mentioned or have not appeared in a photograph please add your name here and maybe stick in a picture to remind you and your family of your contribution to good times in Hotwells.

ACKNOWLEDGMENTS

With grateful thanks to the following for their help and encouragement:

Bristol Museums, Galleries and Archives, Bristol City Library, Bristol University Theatre Collection, Hotwells and Cliftonwood Community Association, Clifton & Hotwells Improvement Society, Clifton Rocks Railway, Hotwells, Clifton and Cliftonwood Local History Society, All the Pantomime people, Living Memories of Hotwells, Steve Stunt, John Parke, Gill Loats, David Burns, Sue Otty, Shirley Brown, Anthea Bruges, Peter Lord, David Brown, Pauline Barnes, Francis Greenacre, Di Steeds, Mary Fuller, Katherine Martin, Chris Bond and Hope Community Church, Maggie Shapland, Peter Davey, Liz Marleyne...
And especially Clive Burlton and Joe Burt of Bristol Books.

FURTHER READING

A History of Clifton by Donald Jones (Phillimore & Co Ltd, 1992)

The Georgian Buildings of Bristol by Walter Ison (Faber & Faber, 1952)

The Bristol Hotwell by Vincent Waite (Bristol Branch of the Historical Association, 1960)

From Bristol to the Sea by Francis Greenacre (Sansom & Company, 2005)

Brunel's Bristol by Angus Buchanan & Michael Williams (Redcliffe Press Ltd, 1982)

Mr Hilhouse of Bristol: Shipbuilder for the Navy 1749-1822 by Andrew Whitefield (Redcliffe Press Ltd, 2010)

Bristol And How It Grew by Dorothy Brown (Bristol Visual & Environmental Group, 1975)

On the Waterfront: The Hotwells Story by Helen Reid and Sue Stops (Redcliffe Press Ltd, 2002)

The Port of Bristol by Andy King (Tempus, 2003)

The Little Book of Bristol by Maurice Fells (The History Press, 2015)

Annals of Bristol in the 17/18/19th centuries by John Latimer

My Bit of Bristol by local personalities (Bristol Evening Post 1988)

PICTURE CREDITS

Frontispiece: Martin Parr
Page 8/9: Bristol Museums, Galleries & Archives, K2386
Page 10: Donald Jones
Page 12: Matthew Directory of Bristol, 1793
Page 13: Emma Marshall 'Bristol Diamonds'
Page 14: Lancaster Maritime Museum
Page 20: Bristol Magpie, 1884
Page 21: Private collection
Page 22: Bristol Archives, RefNo 43207/17/29
Page 23: Peter Davey
Page 24: Bristol Archives, RefNo 43207/9/29/16
Page 25: Denny Long
Page 26: Maurice Mitchell
Page 27: Mrs. Mary Stacey and Maurice Mitchell
Page 30: Bristol Archives, stills from BROFA 0037
Page 32: Kenneth Stradling
Page 33: Symonds Aerial Pictures
Page 35: Symonds Aerial Pictures
Page 37: Liz Marleyne
Page 38: Cartoons by David Brown
Page 48: Les Agar
Page 58: Photos Margo Price, Morph courtesy of Peter Lord
Page 60: John Stops
Pages: 15/17/18/19/30/31/39/40 are Hotwells 2000 images from the Millennium exhibition.
Pages: 45/47 62/63/64/65/66/67/68/69/ 70/71/72/73/74/75/76/77/78 are from Hotwells Pantomime records.
Pages: 53/56/57 are from Hope Centre records.

Whilst every attempt has been made to trace the source of the images, many were given by local people for the Millennium Exhibition. We apologise if we have made any mistakes.